The Path to God's Heart

For my wife,
Barbara, and for all the social workers
so sincerely involved in
teaching India's beggars
'The Prayer of Stillness'

Bernard Huber

The Path to God's Heart

Finding Inwardness in a World of Distractions

Translated by
Patricia Ann Henrich

Cover Note
This book was written for those who have lost what they once had, and for those who are still searching, to help them start out along a path which will lead them to where their own heart longs to be—within the Heart of God.
Cover illustration by Heidi Widmer

© 2011 Bernard Huber
Layouted, printed and published by:
Books on Demand GmbH, Norderstedt, Germany
ISBN: 978-3-8423-9668-5

Contents

Introduction by the Author   7

Part One   11
   A Christian Enlightening   11
   Astonished at the Effect   11
   What Is Stillness?   12
   The Roots of Prayer   16
   Let Christ's Light Shine upon You; Be Enlightened!   18
   Focusing on Christ Will Change Us   21
   The Fruits of Enlightenment   24

Part Two   31
   Awakening   31
   New Depth for My Spiritual Life   31
   Leaving the Dark Side of Life Behind   32
   Making Decisions   36
   Taking Time   39
   Arise, Shine; for Thy Light Is Come!   43
   Being God's Child   46
   Returning to the Heart   48
   Seeking God Only   50

Part Three   55
   Practical Information, Instructions, and Advice   55
   Learning a Lesson from the Beggars   55

Part Four   63
   God Is All Around Us   63
   A Child Begins to Meditate   63
   Daily Practice; The Need for Inner Composure   63
   Learning to Depend upon the Grace of God Only   64
   A Change in Disposition   65

Gaining Vision: Clarity of Thought and Purpose   67

Part Five   70
   Do We Really Need the Prayer of Stillness in Our Daily Lives?70
   Stop and Think about It!   72

Part Six   73
   Attaining the Goal—A Course in Four Stages   73
   Introduction   73

Bibliography   98

Endnotes   100

Introduction by the Author

"I would truly like to believe, but the Christian faith seems to be rather on the abstract side. It doesn't seem to have much to say about my everyday troubles. I'm not really too sure that it means anything much to me personally. On the other hand, what Jesus taught really does make good sense. Take the Sermon on the Mount, for example; if everyone kept to those basic principles, our world would be a totally different place! The big problem is that I just cannot imagine where I would ever be able to get the strength and inner conviction to put those principles into practice."

"I dream of attaining freedom, joy, security, and self-control, but I don't seem to be able to find any one form of spirituality which fulfils my expectations. It seems that certain age groups are attracted to the more modern styles, whereas others tend towards old, but familiar, traditions. As for me, I am on the lookout for something which suits my own personal style."

"There have often been moments when I have felt that what the Bible says about happiness and peace sound wonderful, but that they could never really be meant for me personally."

There are numerous people who might have made these statements or statements similar to them. Many people have felt themselves attracted to the Christian faith; many have even dared giving it a try, only to stumble over the practical points and to end up not knowing how this faith could possibly lead them to the much longed-for and often-promised haven of happiness. Are we aiming too high when we hope to receive a new strength through this new faith—a strength which will support us, comfort, and encourage us? What can we reasonably expect? What will prevent us from losing that first surge of enthusiasm? What will help our faith to grow and to mature? Somewhere deep inside of us, we dream of a powerful faith—a strength flowing from God's inexhaustible springs of clear water—springs which will never run dry, not even as we ourselves grow old.

The idea of writing this book evolved directly from my experiences in India. For several years now, I have been able to observe Indian Christians practising a form of prayer called 'the Prayer of Stillness'. Many years ago, my friend the Reverend Martin Luther and I were able to introduce this particular way of praying to believers in the churches of Southern India. Later, we introduced the same prayer among the beggars living on the streets of India's larger towns. The new Christians in India were experiencing exactly the same problem as christians in western countries have encountered all too often; they wanted to pray but could not concentrate on their prayers. The result was that their faith began to suffer. Many of these Christians were filled with a new eagerness after they had adopted the method of 'stillness'. They acquired an eagerness and a zeal, which has been kept alive to this day. Shepherds and beggars alike, young and old regardless; the countless people who began to seek inner stillness all discovered that it helped their faith to grow deeper and to mature. As we watch the fruits of this form of prayer manifest themselves, we realise that there is adequate reason for taking a closer look at it. The Prayer of Stillness shows us the way to a deeper inwardness. For the people of today's world, who are continually surrounded by distractions, the very idea of there being such a possibility is in itself appealing. Putting this particular way of praying into practise seems quite simple, but we will only find access by constantly keeping our eyes on the goal and our minds on the steps towards it. Only then will we be prepared to set aside the necessary time on a daily basis. We must be prepared to show a certain radical nature in our faith and we must have the willingness to let God change us.

We will have to ask ourselves some important questions: "What is my attitude towards 'time', and how do I make use of 'my time'?"

"Am I good at making decisions?" "What is my attitude towards my own temperament or disposition and towards what I think to be my purpose in life—my mission in life?" This book is for those who want to give God more room in their lives, for those who know intuitively that they can expect to gain more inward joy and peace from a life lived in faith.

The main theme is 'stillness', which means 'without sound or movement'. In Germany and Switzerland, inner stillness is very often associated with 'mysticism', a term which comes from the Greek word '*mystikos*', which means 'mysterious'. Consequently, we often meet with scepticism or mistrust. The Bible, however, uses the words 'mystery' or 'secret' to indicate certain 'truths' to which believers may gain access but which remain hidden from non-believers! The Apostle Paul says that Jesus Christ is 'God's secret' or "the mystery of God."[1] This book is about such 'truths'—truths which will fill the readers with hope and give them the courage to dare to make a fresh start with God, again and again! There is nothing mysterious or mystical about stillness and I shall endeavour to keep the main focus away from 'mystical experiences'. The main focus will be on the beneficial and healing effects of an encounter with God in the inner stillness of our soul. I will refer to some mystics as they must also be given a chance to express their ideas and experiences—a fact which certainly does not mean that I share all their views and convictions. Many of them have made important contributions to Christian spirituality—contributions which cannot merely be ignored.

"Enlighten me, good Jesus, with the brightness of internal light and take away all darkness from the habitation of my heart."
Thomas à Kempis

Part One

A Christian Enlightening

Astonished at the Effect

An Indian bears witness:

I am forty years old. I have lived with my husband in Khairatabad since I was eighteen. When my husband lost his job, we were forced to move to one of the poorest districts of the town. We earned our living by collecting plastic waste, which we then sold. I had been a diligent and eager follower of the god Shiva since my childhood. One day some people from an organisation called 'Bartimaeus Project' visited our district. There were some social workers who came every day to speak to the beggars. They handed out food and clothing, and they taught us personal cleanliness and hygiene. On Sundays, they held a church service where there would be a sermon and prayers. One day I was passing a social worker quite incidentally when I heard him speaking about prayer. I was curious, and so I stood there for a moment listening. I was curious to find out what his understanding of prayer was. Slowly, as I began to get interested in prayer, my doubts vanished. Although I cannot read, one day one of the social workers gave me a booklet called 'The Prayer of Stillness'. He explained what the booklet said about this form of prayer and about the need of having a personal prayer life. I was so impressed that I began to practise this special kind of prayer. I noticed that my way of life was being changed and that I was at peace inwardly.

Hymavathi, Khairatabad

What Is Stillness?

Very many Christians have a deep-seated fear of eastern religions and are therefore very sceptical or mistrustful when confronted with the practice of inner stillness but there are yet others who run the risk of attaching too much significance to that same stillness.

The word 'stillness' comes from the old English words *'stille'* (adjective and adverb) and *'stillan'* (verb) and is of West Germanic origin. It has to do with the absence of all sounds including speech, but it also means 'without movement'. Stillness can lead to an inner silence, which then creates an openness, enabling us to listen and to receive.

A look at the Bible and at Church history will show that stillness has always had an important role to play in Christianity. Stillness has been discovered and rediscovered time and again. Stillness was being practised in monasteries and convents and in various Christian assemblies down through the centuries long before anyone in Europe had ever heard anything of eastern religions. Let us take a look at the role which stillness plays in the Holy Scriptures.

The Bible tells those believers who expect help from God that they should wait in stillness for him to intervene. This period of waiting is not to be thought of as an inactive phase. The believer is now in the best imaginable position, waiting before God, and even while fearing the delay, is making the best possible use of 'time', simply by trusting God's Word and taking it to heart: "Rest in the Lord and wait patiently for him," (literally: "Be still, . . . Enter stillness, . . .")². When we are seeking answers, when we are confused, overburdened, and under great stress, we often run the risk of opening ourselves to all manner of influences. That is when we should pay special attention to what God says in his Word: "These are the words of the Lord God, the Holy One of Israel: Come back, keep peace, and you will be safe; in stillness and in staying

quiet, there lies your strength. But you would have none of it."[3]
Very often, more can be gained by adopting this 'waiting attitude'
than can be gained by many verbally formulated prayers with no
real conviction behind them. Stillness of the soul makes it easier
for us to pray from our hearts. God's Word promises us that the
decisive solution will come, all in good time, and sometimes the
answer is there before we have had to do anything practical about
it ourselves; if only we will adopt an attitude of waiting!

Have you ever found yourself in a situation where you longed for
God to intervene and do something really impressive? The Bible
tells us that God really did appear again and again to prophets
and other specially destined people, and that he appeared in a
spectacular way. In this day and age, contrary to the expectations
of many Christians, God usually comes to us unaccompanied by
blaring trumpets. He comes with a gentle whisper, which can only
be heard by our hearts. The Bible tells us how God came to Elijah
in the wilderness, on Horeb, the mount of God: "The answer came:
Go and stand on the mount before the LORD. For the LORD was
passing by: a great and strong wind came rending mountains and
shattering rocks before him, but the LORD was not in the wind;
and after the wind there was an earthquake, but the LORD was
not in the earthquake; and after the earthquake fire, but the LORD
was not in the fire; and after the fire a low murmuring sound ('a
still, small voice'). When Elijah heard it, he muffled his face in his
cloak and went out and stood at the entrance of the cave. Then
there came a voice . . ."[4]

When God speaks to us during our Prayer of Stillness, we can
compare it to this still, small voice—this gentle whisper. If we are
inwardly quiet and calm, we will discover and develop a new way
of listening; listening with the heart. Each and every person has
moments when they can tune into God, moments when the 'chan-
nel' to him is free from interference—like a radio signal free from
static. If we are going to hear his voice in his Word, we must be

silent. The essential thing about these moments is not the stillness itself, but that we are longing in our hearts to see God act, and the fact that he really does act. The decision to set aside active thinking and to seek stillness, as practised in the Prayer of Stillness, has a soothing effect on our disposition. This is only of interest because it helps us to focus the whole of our inner attention on God. "You are achieving much when you direct your whole heart towards God. If you continue persistently, you will hear and receive him."[5]

My observations in India have shown me that everywhere where Christians decide to 'be still before God' the most remarkable things happen and a process of change begins.

In the New Testament, no other person than Jesus himself proves the importance of stillness. He spent forty days fasting and praying in the wilderness. In the Gospels According to Matthew and According to Luke we read that he was led by the Holy Spirit to be tempted by the devil.[6] This time of retreat, reflection, and stillness helped Jesus to find out exactly in what ways a 'normal' human being is tempted—an extremely important experience for him. He had aimed from the start at taking his place amongst ordinary people like you and I, who are continually susceptible to temptation. The tempter contested Jesus's conception of himself; he began two of his temptations with the words: "If you are the Son of God . . ." Satan has not changed his tactics; they are exactly the same now as they were then. He aims at stunting the growth of self-assurance, and at hindering the development of a sense of identity among God's children.

It is quite clear from what Matthew and Luke tell us that throughout the temptations, the evil one's sole aim was to make Jesus redefine his mission and concentrate on gaining favour amongst his fellow citizens. The idea was to entice Jesus to do wonders and display his power, thereby gaining admiration and applause from the people around him. Such approval must indeed generate a feeling of happiness and a sense of self-esteem. Jesus found himself in a situation which is familiar to most of us as a part of our everyday lives!

If Jesus had succumbed to those temptations, he would have become egocentric, just like the rest of us. He would not have been able to walk the path which finally led to salvation for all mankind. Personally, I cannot imagine how Jesus would have been able to walk that very same path to inwardness, surrounded by the noise and tumult of one of our modern-day cities.

In the wilderness, he could perceive the kind of struggle that we, as mere humans, are confronted with. He summoned up the strength to fulfil his mission together with God the Father. He discovered for himself in his capacity as God's Son, the complete triviality of everything material or superficial. In fact, his Word often warns us of the dangers involved in overvaluing material things. He entered a more profound freedom than any other person has ever experienced, and so was able to sacrifice himself for the world. If we sometimes wonder where the source of his credibility lies, we must seek it above all in his absolute selflessness.

The writers of the Gospels tell us that Jesus (often) ". . . went away to a lonely spot and remained there in prayer."[7] His call to radical discipleship encourages us to keep going, and words such as: "So also none of you can be a disciple of mine without parting with all his possessions."[8] ceaselessly draw our attention to the fundamentals.

If we really want to find the deepest truths of life, we will need a place where we can come close to God and to ourselves—a place of mutual 'communication'. Do we really believe that we will be able to find these truths in any other way? Do we believe that we will be able to overcome the enemies in us and around us through any other means?

The Apostle Paul's path was similar when he went off to Arabia.[9] Before Paul began his apostolic work, he sought deeper fellowship with God in the seclusion of the wilderness. The desired and ultimate goal of meditants[10] practising the Prayer of Stillness should be to eventually reach an inner freedom, which will enable them to confess in the words of Paul: "I have been crucified with Christ: the life I now live is not my life, but the life which Christ lives in me."[11]

The Prayer of Stillness needs no theological justification. It is important for us to realise, as Jesus realised, just exactly what God is demanding of us when he says: "Love the Lord your God with all your heart, with all your soul, with all your strength, and with all your mind."[12] No one needs to justify themselves for seeking God 'with all their heart' in the stillness of their soul. For many Christians, for those who wish to draw near to God, there is very likely no alternative, and there is almost certainly no other way of seeking him than 'with all your heart'.

Food for thought:
– *What is your attitude towards stillness? Have you had any previous experience with stillness?*
– *What helps you to recognise how God sees you and how he sees your present situation?*
– *Can you believe that God has specific plans for your future?*

The Roots of Prayer

The most important thing about the Prayer of Stillness is not, as we have already said, the stillness itself, it is a striving and a longing in our hearts, which makes it easier for us to come closer to God. Our innermost wish is to escape from the continual distractions which take our minds off prayer. Distractions rob us of the inner quietude necessary for concentration and so keep us from hearing Christ's words. As we attempt to come closer to Christ through self-denial,[13] stillness serves us as a tool—as a mere means of achieving the goal. In Christian mysticism, exactly as in the teachings of Jesus, self-denial is looked upon as the attribute which will be of most help to us as we strive to come closer to God. On the surface, the Prayer of Stillness looks much the same as the 'silent prayer' or 'quiet prayer' as practised and rediscovered time and again in Christian mysticism throughout the centuries. The silent or quiet prayer is based on an ancient, traditional Christian form of prayer, which was practised in the western world at a time when nothing was known of the forms of meditation, later to be 'imported' from the Far East, and which now enjoy so much approval almost everywhere. Johannes Cassian,[14] who mentions it in his writings, learnt to pray this way from the desert fathers of the Egyptian deserts as early as in the fourth century. Provided the aim of stillness is to listen and wait for God's voice, the Prayer of Stillness must be understood as a Christian alternative or response to eastern mysticism and, therefore, the two should not be mingled together. The Prayer of Stillness has been developed as a Christian practice in its own right, and the difference between it and classical theology is that it is accessible to people from all walks of life, in the present day, just as it was thousands of years ago. This kind of mysticism, which leads to Christian hearing and acting, has its roots in the teachings of the Bible. The protestant mystic Gerhard Tersteegen quite correctly called the patriarchs of the Old Testament 'true mystics'. The theology of prayer borrows the principle of 'stillness' from conceptions to be found in the mystical theology of bygone centuries, and so helps those who pray to experience God at a deeper level. Each individual will have to discover for themselves as to what extent this form of prayer actually helps them in their own lives.

The Prayer of Stillness is not, first and foremost, a way of resolving conflicts and is not to be confused with any form of psychotherapy. We have, however, noticed that when people practising this form of prayer, listen to God and his Word, a process leading to a positive change begins to work in their lives.

Let Christ's Light Shine upon You; Be Enlightened!

Divine enlightenment or 'inspiration', in this sense, is the result of either having undergone a process of spiritual training and development, or it is the result of a mystical experience having opened the door for the believer leading them directly to God's grace. Other religions accentuate the first way, whereas Christian mysticism lays the emphasis on the Grace of God (ie: free pardon), through which we may approach Christ.

Decisive is that we let God's light enter our lives. The Apostle Paul wrote as follows: "Awake thou that sleepest, and arise from the dead, and Christ shall give thee light."[15] The Apostle equates 'life' (i.e. arising from the dead) with 'coming to the light' or 'walking in the light'. Paul knows that there is a Christian enlightenment—a Christian inspiration. If we want to concentrate wholly on Christ, our part is to let go of anything and everything that could hinder us from following him. His light will show us our own special encumbrances: "Bad men all hate the light and avoid it, for fear their practices should be shown up. The honest man comes to the light so that it may be clearly seen that God is in all he does."[16] When, in stillness of the soul, we allow all our thoughts to come to the surface instead of suppressing them, we are doing the equivalent of looking at our lives day by day—exactly as we look at ourselves in a mirror. The Apostle John had no doubt whatsoever that walking in the light also includes loving the brethren. Listen to what he says: "But one who hates his brother is in the darkness; he walks in the darkness and has no idea where he is going, because the darkness has made him blind."[17]

The burdens under which we suffer are quite often things which we are not even prepared to admit to ourselves; we are not capable of acknowledging them as burdens. Remedies such as concentrating our intellect on the Bible or on the sacraments; leaning on other crutches such as the teachings of our own particular church, even relying on our own dogged opinions and methods may help at times, but as remedies they will all turn out to be inadequate and unsatisfactory in the end. They very often hold us back when we should be striving on towards Christ and setting the liberating power of his Gospel into action.

Even a traditional, intellectualistic, or rationalistic theology (a theology derived wholly from pure reason) is of limited help. Gerhard Tersteegen said: "It is foolishness to seek knowledge and understanding of God and his truth by means of the effectiveness of reason."[18] In truth and in reality, the power and appeal of the Christian faith lies in the fact that it is this very faith which helps us to gain experience and make progress in our discipleship of Christ! Only then can God shed his light on us, revealing our spiritual blindness.

This is why John speaks of 'being enlightened': "The real light which enlightens every man was even then coming into the world."[19] He meant the salvation which comes from faith in Christ, but undoubtedly, he also meant the ability to let go of everything that turns us into the helpless victims of all kinds of outside influence: victims of advertising, of temptations, and of our own imagination. The Apostle Paul speaks of a light which God commanded to shine out of the darkness and which ". . . hath shined in our hearts, to give the light of the knowledge of the glory of God in the face of Jesus Christ."[20] He means the hearts of all people; our hearts should be literally 'seized' by the light so that we may really come to know God and so reach a point where we see God and ourselves with clarity.

It is, in fact, a matter of becoming aware of the presence of Christ in our own lives and of being able to perceive his guidance. Right at the beginning of the Bible we are told about the Israelites' exodus from Egypt to the Wilderness of Sin (which is between Elim and Sinai) four thousand years ago: "The Lord went before them by day in a pillar of cloud, to lead them the way; and by night in a pillar of fire, to give them light; to go by day and night . . .,"[21]. It is in a very similar way that the 'enlightened ones' are led by God through the 'wilderness of life'. Nowadays, we are not only led by outward signs, but also inwardly through the presence of Christ, his Word, and his Spirit within us. Light enters into our lives through God because God himself is light. It is not at all surprising that Jesus said of himself: "I am the light of the world." Christian enlightenment (inspiration) always happens in connection with Jesus, who is the Living Word.

As we move more and more within the sphere of his light, our own lives will become brighter and clearer. The time we spend in the Prayer of Stillness is also a time in which we learn to look at ourselves. We begin to see many things in a way in which we never saw them before as we gradually learn to see our motives and our various trains of thought from God's point of view. Naturally, these changes will only come about if we are prepared to listen constantly to the Word of God, which means reading the Holy Scriptures. What could be better? Jesus speaks about 'coming to his light', whereby those seeking God do not shrink from learning the truth about themselves and their lives. Those who seek sincerely need have no fear: "The honest man comes to the light so that it may be clearly seen that God is in all he does."[22]

Living in the light has something fascinating about it! We let go of all that hinders us; at the same time our talents begin to unfold and develop, and our lives suddenly take on a new quality that was not there before—a quality appropriate to our true calling. In most cases, this involves a process whereby the person praying is led forward step by step.

Food for thought:
– To what extent does your faith rest on things which you have personally experienced or on opinions and views adopted from others?

– Are you prepared to allow God to work on you and change you through his Gospel?

Focusing on Christ Will Change Us

It is not a special meditative technique that sets off this transformation; it is God who begins working on us as soon as we focus on Christ. What we are striving to gain through stillness is not a state whereby our minds cease to be actively occupied with thoughts; it is a quietness in which we focus on Jesus in the absence of words or thoughts! We should not think of our times of devotion, our quiet times of prayer, in terms of being 'a means to an end' (in German: 'purpose and fulfilment'). Friso Melzer was perfectly right when he said: "Those who, when contemplating meditation, make a satisfactory answer a condition of their decision (i.e. the decision as to whether to meditate or not), would not be capable of mediation. Should they nevertheless attempt it, their efforts would be without fruit . . . If meditation indeed has no actual purpose, it is still not meaningless or pointless. Even if meditation offers no fulfilment, what it does do is to bring fruit."[23] All that counts is that we strive to get closer to Christ and his will. The conscious act of surrendering ourselves to him again, and yet again, will have a liberating effect on our lives. What then follows is worth infinitely more than anything which we could achieve by relying on our own resources. While we are silent and when we 'let go', we ". . . seek his face."[24] And what do we see?—The picture of Christ crucified, who wholly renounced his own self and then so completely identified himself with us that he was willing to take our sins upon himself. It is not for nothing that we read: "He did not think to snatch equality with God, but made himself nothing, assuming the nature of a slave. Bearing the human likeness, revealed in human shape, he humbled himself . . ."[25]

A key characteristic of the Prayer of Stillness is Christ's complete devotion, which makes us want to identify ourselves with him only, and to become like him in inner quietude and reflection! He let go of everything for our sakes. It is our desire to behold him and through beholding we will soon find that `letting go` becomes possible.

We will notice how he ". . . makes his face to shine upon us . . ." Just exactly what proportion of this inner transformation is done by the person praying and what is carried out by God alone has often been a matter of debate amongst us. One thing is certain: It is God who, through his Holy Spirit, brings about the desired change which leads to the breakthrough of grace. He pours out his healing whenever a genuine encounter with him takes place.

It is not even necessary for us to try and imagine which subsequent or 'new' levels our 'prayer' is leading us to. The key characteristic of the Prayer of Stillness is not that we 'do' something, but that we wait expectantly for something to 'happen' to us. Our part is to turn back from our own 'do-it-yourself' type ways—ways which generally lead to a dark abyss.

The Indian mystic Sadhu Sundar Singh describes this adeptly in a dialogue between a saint and a philosopher: "Once the philosopher asked the saint: 'You truly believe that you are helping others by sitting here silently praying?' The saint answered: '. . . My meaning (intention or purpose) is clear. God works in silence. No man has ever heard him speak or make any sound. To hear his voice, we must wait for him in silence. Then, without voice or words, he will speak to the soul in the secret room of the heart. As he himself is spirit, he addresses the soul in spiritual language, fills it with his presence, and finally revives and refreshes it forever.' "[26]

Once asked about his qualifications in theology, this Indian mystic answered as follows: "When I spend many hours in contemplation,[27] I find enlightenment (inspiration), and God reveals to me so many things that I am not able to express them

22

all in my own language. We have learnt some theology, but God is the source of all divine knowledge. In this manner I can learn things within seconds for which I would otherwise have needed years to understand."[28]

Do you feel that the goal is set too high? The times when nothing 'special' happens for a while, or when we experience relapses instead of making progress, those are precisely the times to wait patiently for God; he never comes too late. We have to assume that God has his own time plan for each one of us and that he will, in the end, achieve what his will for us is. He will reach the goal(s) that he wants to reach with us, provided we are willing to reach those same goal(s) with him. Until that time comes, most of us have a great deal to catch up on in the realms of trusting God, and of inner healing and practical obedience concerning his Word. If we open our hearts and let God in, we will see that an appreciable amount of the 'time' representing our lives must serve as a preparation period for the important things which are yet to come. During this whole process of maturing everything, even set-backs and defeats, serves to help us along our own particular path of faith. This process can only be speeded up by the continual practice of trusting Christ and giving ourselves completely to him.

J. Tauler stresses that ". . . (as) they know that Christ has his own time; a time when he will enlighten (inspire) them, they abandon themselves calmly to his will."[29] God would like to give us everything all at once, but we need time to open ourselves to his gifts, ". . . by making our small contribution we build, together with God, the reciprocal loving relationship between us and him for which we were created."[30]

Food for thought:
– To what extent have healing changes in your life been brought about by prayer and reading the Holy Scriptures?

— What changes to your character and your ability to trust God are you currently going through? What changes are you striving for?

The Fruits of Enlightenment

Generally speaking, we can say that there are certain outward similarities between the different forms of meditation practised in various cultures, and that meditation is usually accompanied by the same kind of visible signs. In most cases, meditants follow the rules established for their own particular form of meditation; the body becomes less tense; i.e. muscles relax, blood pressure becomes normal; heartbeat and breathing become calmer and more regular. One also notices that the meditant has a more even and well-balanced temperament and is more able to remain calm in stressful situations.

The Prayer of Stillness also has the effect of liberating us from the continual distractions which lead our minds astray when praying. Such distractions are not to be underestimated; they are a considerable hindrance when our desire is to hear Christ's Word and to make progress in our spiritual lives.

Let us understand what it is to liberate our own will. When we turn to Christ and seek stillness, the attractions of the 'outside' world can no longer influence us enough to monopolise us completely. If we succumb to a temptation, our heart usually bonds itself with the object of that temptation. It becomes so completely monopolised that our will is for all practical purposes 'faded-out' like the end of a transmission, and we take no more notice of it. It is as if our will were literally blinded, and so the temptation gains control over our very nature; over our disposition, and our thoughts. The Bible tells us that "temptation has its roots in a man's (or a woman's) own lust."[31] The more we seek Christ in stillness and follow in his footsteps, the less our thoughts and actions will be controlled by the images which outside attractions are so good at conjuring up inside us.

Those who do not choose to go through this process of change will never be entirely aware of their own imperfections; they will see them only to a very small degree. Increasing remoteness from God is not usually a disturbing enough factor in their lives to make them wish to seek gradual changes and therefore to change their whole situation. In many cases, the will of God even appears to be somehow veiled while our own will is paralysed. The result is that we cannot understand what we are missing by not following Christ. We grieve very little (or not at all) over the time we are wasting, the strength we do not receive, and the opportunities which we throw away without so much as a second thought. Neither do we spare a thought to worry about the effects on our lives that such an attitude will almost certainly have. We often identify ourselves with thoughts, intentions, and actions which we claim we really want to reject, although we are often not even prepared, let alone willing, to remove ourselves from the sphere of their influence! Just that can happen when we are immersed in a television programme. We accept, passively and without uttering a word, the influence which this media exerts on us, even when we insist that we do not, in any way, agree with the messages that are conveyed. It is in the nature of sin to rob us of our ability to recognise the truth and to take the edge off our astuteness before we realise what is happening!

During the Prayer of Stillness, our orientation is geared towards Jesus; such orientation is a good remedy against the spiritual lethargy which likes to creep in on us when we mediate. In a state of stillness, meditants are in a position to observe themselves and become aware of their own blindness and so they can begin to gauge the consequences of their attitudes and behaviour.

The ultimate objective is to give our hearts the right orientation, and in stillness allow Christ to fulfil his purpose. This practice brings about such changes in a person's disposition that meditants will find that they are very soon encouraged to allow the process more and more space and time in their lives. They become aware of their own progress and notice a certain cleansing effect on their inner lives. Benedict of Canfield ascribes a cleansing attribute to the love which arises from this relationship: ". . . so that all imperfections fade away and disappear; are completely shattered."[32] Whereas the conflicts of temptation struggling within us will often neutralise our will, meditants will now find themselves in a position to receive strength from God—strength to do what they had been wanting to do all along—the strength to receive the Word of God in their hearts.

Experience has taught us that the needs of each individual person vary. Some will go through this process quite quickly, while others will take longer to arrive at the goal. Merely recognising the powers which harm us will help us to see our faults more clearly, but that does not mean that we have already won the battle! Genuine inner changes are usually the result of a somewhat longer process. With the passing of time the authenticity and depth of the transformation will be recognisable by its fruits. Meditants must be continually encouraged to give their undivided attention to the presence of the Lord Jesus and to allow that presence to fill them more and more.

Learning to let go of everything else will help them to discover how very close Christ really is. If at first, they had thought that the only thing needed was to seek him actively, they will later notice that whether they find him or not is wholly dependent upon their inner attitude. He is always ready to reveal himself! The words of Zechariah quite clearly point the way: "Come close to God, and he will come close to you."[33] Christ, who stands 'as slumbering' at our side, the very same Christ who has taken up his abode within us, is waiting to be noticed, waiting for us to call upon him, waiting for us to listen to his Words: "Enlightenment comes when the meditant desires nothing more than what is God's will, so that God no longer needs to isolate himself from our wants and desires."[34] When our *only* desire is for God's will, God can trust us to want nothing *outside* his will.

The Lord Jesus talks to us in the Gospels about close relationships. He even talks of belonging to a spiritual family. He says: "My mother and my brothers (and sisters)—they are those who hear the word of God and act upon it."[35] Jesus finds it of the utmost importance for us that we should act upon what we have heard. He wants to enter into a closeness between himself and all creatures, a closeness paraphrased in the following words: "Anyone who loves me will heed what I say; then my Father will love him, and we will come to make our dwelling with him."[36] Our heeding, or hearing, should not be restricted by any biased thoughts or negative attitudes.

The Prayer of Stillness offers the necessary setting—a place where our hearts can learn to have an attitude of heeding and obeying. Even if the word 'obedience' has practically vanished from the area of spiritual activities nowadays; it deserves to be enhanced in the area of discipleship. Relating to our relationship to Christ, we must be completely sure that there can be no better way to follow than his way; the way he himself chooses. Only then, will we voluntarily decide to link our will to Christ's will.

When this happens, we need no longer identify ourselves with negative emotions or with thoughts that only serve to harm us; we are on the way to reaching that state of freedom which enables us to see the will of Christ as being our very own will. We are no longer forced to say: "I live in fear, I cannot break free of my own negative temperament, and I have no choice but to do evil, even though I condemn it. I am full of hatred." Even if we have never before been able to submit to God's Word without a great effort, even if God's Word alone was never enough, and we have always had to supplement our spiritual lives with explanatory and edifying literature, God's Word is suddenly made accessible through stillness alone.

At any time in our day-to-day lives, we are able to find our way back to the same spiritual state of mind which we experienced when we surrendered ourselves to God in the Prayer of Stillness. It is the very essence of our daily experience which allows us the freedom. It is a welcome state into which we can enter again and again, despite the pressure and strain of everyday situations and the numerous and varying influences with which we are bombarded. We will have to practise and develop this technique in much the same way as any other skill must be learnt. Factors such as fatigue or the power which our ingrained ways of thinking and behaviour patterns still hold over us play an important role. We may make brilliant progress, but we will, nevertheless, remain imperfect and dependent upon God's grace alone.

The fruit of enlightenment is wide and varied. As soon as we shed more and more of the things which have been keeping us from seeing and hearing Christ through our spiritual senses, we will begin to notice how willing he is to mould and shape us. As Teresa of Avila stated quite emphatically: "It is extremely important that people who have begun to practise inward prayer should, at the same time, begin to practise ridding themselves of all kinds of gratification."[37] She does not mean that we must do without all the things that make our lives pleasant, nor does she mean the joy that we gain when we share our lives with others. She means the obstacles which slow us down or even bring us to a grinding halt. We may best overcome our inner enemies by inwardly turning away from them and then turning towards the Lord Jesus. Both acts; turning away from those things which harm us and turning towards Christ, must be practised continually in the stillness of our prayer. The first and foremost conscious act of praying is giving ourselves to Christ, and the next is self-denial. Through experience after experience, we will realise that by adopting this mode of behaviour we can only stand to gain, and we will have the necessary motivation to keep moving forward along the path we have started out on.

Why do so many people expect so much in answer to their short, often insincere, prayers, and the few hastily read Bible verses they have just managed to snatch time for? They wonder why so little happens. Do we really have to wonder why faith remains barren in the lives of those who do not understand that faith must be accompanied by times of soul-searching, times of reflection and stillness?

If a person genuinely searches their own soul, they will soon notice that being completely at God's disposal is more than worth-while because God's desire is the same: He wants to be there, within our reach at all times. The conventional, often totally in-adequate and misrepresented image of a Christ,—which pictures him as some kind of 'dear old matey', whose only purpose is to stand at our side, forever ready to help, or (the other extreme), as a Christ who cannot possibly be approached by mere mortals,— differs greatly from the picture of a merciful and holy God who is waiting patiently to create a better life, a better environment, and a better world, not only for us, but with us. Christ is always with us, and he is waiting to help us move forward.

Meditants encounter God in the Prayer of Stillness on a daily basis and so find it easier to live a life in accordance with God's will. They notice that ways and means are now openly available to them—means which they had previously had little or no knowl-edge of. They had been hindered by distraction, fear, and fatigue, which indeed had been rooted in their own oppressive and often bleak thoughts and which had never ceased to rob them of their strength and paralyse their minds. They suddenly become aware of God's presence, and standing in that presence they begin to trust his Word and to await his help. They become more and more able to remember and to treasure God's Word, consequently their whole way of thinking and their freedom of choice is set free; liberated. They no longer feel committed to any kind of constraint or fear, because they feel committed to Jesus Christ alone. They can begin to use hitherto wasted, unused, or even misused energy to develop their life's work and visions. It is amazing just to see the amount of imagination and energy that develops in Christians who abide in Christ and open their hearts and minds to his presence and to his Word.

Food for thought:
– *How much 'spiritual light' do you allow to enter daily into your life?*
– *How close to Christ do you feel?*
– *How do you go about making sure that the words of the Holy Scriptures can really influence the way you think, speak, and act?*

"Christian self-denial is only the beginning of a divine fulfilment.
It is inseparable from the inward conversion of our whole being
from ourselves to God. It is the denial of our unfulfilment,
the renunciation of our own poverty."[38]
Thomas Merton

Part Two

Awakening

New Depth for My Spiritual Life

An Indian bears witness:

The Prayer of Stillness is especially suited to people whose desire is for more depth to their faith and who wish fervently to follow Christ. I kept asking myself the same things: How could I increase my faith and what would my future life with Christ be like?

I had never thought that it would be a form of prayer, a prayer so totally linked to stillness, which would show me the way, yes, finally point me in the right direction. Very soon, after I had started, I noticed how my fellowship with the Holy Trinity, that is, with God the Father, the Son, and the Holy Spirit, was growing deeper in a very special way. I discovered that I was really experiencing the things that I had been promised about the Prayer of Stillness. I discovered anew just what it is like to know God as a Father, and what it is like to focus on doing the will of the Holy Spirit.

Important things, things which I had always been familiar with, but things which I had never paid much attention to, suddenly began to take on a real importance in my own life—things, such as inner peace and joy and God's righteousness. I became newly aware of the strength that was mine—strength that faith alone endued me with.

Gradually, something started to happen in my life. My faith became more steadfast and more resolute. The more the Prayer of Stillness grew to be a habit with me, the more joy I got from my daily encounters with God. I was somehow revived. I literally took a more active interest in life, and I gained a kind of freedom in my life as a Christian which I had never known before. Since then I have been telling others about the strength and the power; about what a person stands to gain through the Prayer of Stillness. It is very difficult to put all the things that I have gained into words.

S. S. Mohanty, Bhubaneshwar

Leaving the Dark Side of Life Behind

We could say a great deal about the dark side of life. We become aware of the existence of a dark side in many different ways; through fear, failure, anxieties, or through negative thinking. These sensations are all only the symptoms of a deep inner loneliness and isolation. They are also quite clearly the cause of a negative disposition, which in turn can quite often result in a tendency to addictive behaviour.

We quite naturally like to blame outside influences for our own inner restlessness and our anxieties. Most of the time we are not well-equipped enough, at least not inwardly, to overcome our dark side or to cope with our own private inner darkness. Sometimes we cannot even recognise exactly what 'things' are making us feel so troubled, so anxious . . . and if we do recognise them, we very often refuse to admit that they trouble us! We resign ourselves, and learn to live with them as if they were an intrinsic part of our lives. If we accept these unnamed forces as unavoidable; if we begin to believe that they are a part of our personality and that we cannot hope to change anything, they will win the final victory. Then, in our helplessness, we make out that our bad habits are really 'virtues'. It is easier to join forces with an enemy when he seems to have the upper hand than it is to put up some kind of a fight. Present-day society does the same thing when it legalises behaviour or deeds which had hitherto been illegal, but which can no longer be kept under control as people in general no longer consider them to be wrong or repulsive. That is one way of neatly resolving the problem, but it is only a short-term solution.

The good thing is that we are continually invited to turn back and start again because no situation is beyond hope of change. During our time of stillness our own ability to let God's grace take charge of our lives causes hope to stir within us. This hope begins to grow putting out tender shoots and showing us that God has new and better things in store for us. This is the exact opposite to our never-ending attempts at getting our dark side under control. It is that dark side which wants to lead us back into sinful ways. Letting go and focusing on Christ gives us a new vision for the inexhaustible possibilities that we now have access to through God's Holy Spirit.

How do we move forward and finally enter God's light? How do we reach the point where we have a greater knowledge of ourselves and of God? An encounter with our own subconscious mind is integral to the Prayer of Stillness. Encountering God makes us able to ". . . understand something which would remain hidden from us if we were intent on seeing it only through conscious thinking."[39]

There is practically always a moment in time during the Prayer of Stillness when we have to stop and think about our own guilt, our incorrect, or even bad behaviour, and the impurities of our character. The only thing to do when this moment comes is to remember Christ's grace and his forgiveness, and to remember how they are expressed in the Baptism of Faith. Consciously letting go of everything else, only to walk with Christ in his path, is in itself proof that 'the person who we once were' has died, and that we really wish 'to live only unto God, in union with Jesus Christ.'

Many people wonder why they are so unsure about the forgiveness of their sins. They do not seem to realise that this very forgiveness must be accepted deep in the human heart through hearing God's Word before it can become effective. By letting go of everything we create a void, which waits to be filled by the Word of God. If forgiveness is only seen as wishful thinking, or if it is only accepted on an intellectual level—perhaps in connection with some kind of traditional liturgy—then there will never be absolute certainty, and we will never know for sure that we are forgiven.

Then again, we must emphasise that we do not expect any change to occur simply through this particular form of prayer. We expect Christ to effect the change. We continue praying, always relying totally on the grace of Christ, until we notice that a change for the better has been set in motion. Sometimes the transfer of power is a prolonged process, in which case, we should look for the reasons behind this delay in our own heart. We are very often still in love with our negative disposition, or we cannot let go of a favourite sin. When we speak of sin, we do so without meaning to put a person in a negative light. What the Bible has to say about sin only shows how much God loves mankind. We do not like to admit to ourselves that we alone are to blame when we suffer defeats or when the process of change is a long-drawn-out one.

We are often very slow in becoming aware of the opportunities, of the chances, and of the ways and means open to us. If we understood how to engender change more immediately, we would be able to prevent quite a number of defeats and many a catastrophe. Many people undergo a certain weakening of character under the ruthless influence of the media, which makes it essential that they concentrate far more on inwardness and the things of the spirit as an effective means of offering resistance. We thoroughly agree with Thomas à Kempis, who said that 'silence and inner calmness' are the best tools with which to reach that very same goal.

Can you remember ever having been in a situation where you

asked God to help you to do his will and then realised that you did not have the strength to accomplish what you had asked? On many occasions, the reason for our lack of strength is the fact that we do not know how to go about the necessary soul-searching allowing God and his Holy Spirit to carry out their works in us. Ours is a culture based on intellect; it does not allow us easy access to our own hearts, which makes it extremely difficult, if not altogether impossible, for God's Word to take root in our hearts and bear fruit. Among other things, the Prayer of Stillness aims at regaining inwardness—a goal which makes certain changes unavoidable.

It is a sad fact that prayer, which is our best 'weapon' when it comes to conquering our inner lives, occupies only the tiniest place in the lives of the inhabitants of the western world. Countless people have grown accustomed to a spiritual life trimmed down almost to non-existence. They invest about as much time as it takes to keep them spiritually afloat. We like to speak of the 'Christian five- to ten-minute Prayer'. The trouble is that to experience the necessary fundamental changes, we need to have more than a superficial encounter with Christ; we need the kind of deep and lasting daily encounters with him and his Word which will lead us towards a new vision for our lives.

Food for thought:
– *Are there things which have a disturbing effect on your life; things which you long ago ceased to struggle against, because you saw no way of ever changing them?*
– *Do you feel, deep inside of you, a disposition or a temperament, which is tormenting you and robbing you of your strength?*
– *Do you believe and trust that God can bring about the changes in your life that you are longing for?*

Making Decisions

Our faith and our progress along the path of our lives is primarily influenced and directed by the decisions we make. In the course of our day-to-day lives, we can usually manage to compensate for what we have neglected or completely failed to do, without causing much damage! The really big decisions in life, such as: "What do I want to devote my life to?"—"What are my innermost convictions; my beliefs?"—"What are my goals; my aims?" are not as easy to put off; not as easy to ignore. Could we possibly be unaware of the consequences; totally ignorant of what will happen should we fail to make such important decisions? We are even less aware of the spiritual 'war' being waged all around us, of the fights and struggles from which we can only emerge as either the conqueror or the conquered.

Many people absorb so much media that they see life as if it were some kind of an enjoyable film—all fun and thrills (without the spills!). Death, and what comes after it, are comparable to the risk such individuals take when they enter, without even hesitating, into a game which they do not take quite seriously despite the high stakes. They do not notice the negative effects which such an attitude has on their view of life neither do they notice that they are failing to make any kind of (spiritual) progress. To put it another way; in such a frame of mind they fail to recognise the seriousness of the question of life and death, and being insufficiently decided in their faith, they trivialise fundamental Biblical truths!

How are we going to summon up the strength necessary to make these decisions? Each of us 'writes' their own scenario for the 'film of their lives' and this is where decisions come in. If we want the story of our life to be staged according to God's script and according to his plan, then we will need to make decisions. Unfortunately, we do not always have the energy needed to take the steps that would bring us closer to God. During the time of stillness meditants are confronted anew with the importance of exercising their will. Even though we cannot change our own nature immediately or without help, we can create the ambient conditions in which not only our desire to become a changed person increases, but also our longing to be close to God grows.

We are sometimes reminded of the decisions we must make if we want that much longed-for certainty; decisions resulting automatically in the fulfilment of God's promises. For example, a complete certainty that we have the promise of eternal life in heaven can only result from our having accepted the forgiveness of our sins and from our having made a definite decision to follow Christ. Similarly, we can only enter into the peace which the Lord Jesus promised his disciples by faithfully hearing and obeying Christ's Word.

We will not be spared having to deal with decisions concerning fundamental principles. There are situations where we will be confronted with 'either/or' questions, just as Israel was. The prophet Elijah challenges the people of Israel and asks them: "How long will you sit on the fence? If the Lord is God, follow him; but if Baal, then follow him."[40] Israel had to decide whether to worship God or to worship Baal, and during the course of our lives we will be called upon to make many similar decisions. It should be easier for us to make the correct choice than it was for them. God is much closer to us, through his Holy Spirit and his Word, than he was to Israel at that time. Reaching out towards him and his guidance will help us to make even the most difficult decisions.

The answer to the 'either/or' question is one which will influence our whole lives, our mindset and our actions. We will sense God's close proximity if, in the stillness of our souls, we use our powers of decision to decide for God's Word and against all forms of envy, greed, lethargy, impure thoughts, pride, and so on.

The first chapters of the Bible show us that Christ is closer to us than we are to ourselves. Becoming aware of his closeness, and of how we are getting closer to our own selves, is the key to developing our powers of decision. To Cain, who was in danger of being caught up in his own jealousy, God says: "If thou doest well, shalt thou not be accepted? And if thou doest not well, sin lieth at the door. And unto thee shall be his desire, and thou shalt rule over him."[41] Thus we can see that there is no point in trying to make out that we are not responsible for making decisions. If we try to wriggle out of decision-making, our goal will only become even more remote, and we will consequently have less chance of reaching it.

There is a certain amount of space within which we can be ourselves. We call this space 'our own free will', and it represents the space between the actual temptation and how we react to it. The space in which we exercise our own free will can be a larger or a smaller area, depending on the general conditions under which we grew up, what sort of a childhood we had, what we experienced in our youth, and the conditions under which we live at present.

The purpose of the Prayer of Stillness is, among other things, that we should learn to use this space more and more often. Day-by-day, we deliberately open our hearts to Christ's presence, and in doing so, we come face to face with him. Daily we draw nearer to accepting that the most profound truth of the Christian faith applies to our own lives; Jesus Christ is God and Lord! This confession, this declaration of faith, first spoken by the Apostle Thomas, flows from deep within us and has an automatically invigorating effect on our lives. Whether or not we manage to translate this into reality will first and foremost, show in our characters. Pious sentiments are usually meant well, but very often they must be classified as mere wishful thinking.

What counts in the long run is not what we claim or wish to be, but alone what we are and what we will become in Christ. This is what Jesus was constantly telling his disciples.

Our future is no longer determined by our circumstances or

by how other individuals have treated us, but it is determined by the decisions which we are now prepared and able to make, and by Christ, who stands by us and by our choices. When we become dependent on God, the promise made by the Apostle Peter is fulfilled: "And the God of all grace . . . will himself, after your brief suffering, restore, establish, and strengthen you on a firm foundation."[42] It is time to rediscover the real purpose and importance of our own will; it is time to commit ourselves to letting go of the things that are holding us back.

Food for thought:
– *What important decisions have you been putting off? What decisions should you not put off any longer?*
– *What attempts have you made to make these decisions? Are their any obstacles hindering you from making another attempt?*
– *Do you feel free to exercise your own will when it comes to doing the good and acceptable thing for God? If so, how free do you feel?*
– *What has most helped you so far to follow Christ?*

Taking Time

If we want to make the right decisions and learn how to see the difference between important and comparatively unimportant matters, we will have to be patient and practise the art of waiting. The time needed for the Prayer of Stillness can be a major obstacle for some people. We can find the time if we really want to! We all have sufficient time and enough opportunities for every step towards progress in our lives. We are on dangerous ground when we claim to have no time for important decisions or for God!

Changes of any great importance do not usually come about unless we are prepared to sacrifice our time for them. They deserve our attention much more than worldly goods or outward appearances because they are concerned with the essentials. Do we not tend to live our everyday lives with one foot in the present and the other in the past or in the future? For example, we are having a meal, and at the same time our thoughts are occupied in such a way with what we are going to be doing later on, that we get no real enjoyment out of the meal! During a conversation, while the other person is actually talking, our mind is busy working out what we are going to say next! We do not even notice that we are missing out on meaningful relationships with our fellow beings. Our bustling activity; our frantic busyness often gets out of control and then it represents a real problem. Many of us have become slaves and fallen victim to 'time'—or to 'lack of time'. One could go so far as to say that we are more at time's disposal than time is at our disposal, and the 'time' which we have been allotted, which is in reality our life, only serves as a means to an end. We 'do' far more than any generation before us could achieve. We are supreme achievers, but we are dismal failures when it comes to putting God and the well-being of our neighbours (our fellow humans) first. We do not even care much about our own 'lives' as such, and in failing to do so, we manage to exclude eternity from our thoughts.

The spiritual significance of 'taking time' is that we begin to live in the present; we become aware of that moment in time which is 'now'. God is always to be found in the present; he is omnipresent. He appears as the one who is, was, and will always be present![43] If, through the wrong attitude and false expectations, we fail to encounter him right here and now where he is always to be found, we are running the risk of being convicted by the words of the Lord Jesus: ". . . they may look and look, but see nothing; they may hear and hear, but understand nothing; otherwise they might turn to God to be forgiven."[44] We will be convicted for the simple reason that we have refused God's offer!

Our notion of what the past, the future, and eternity mean to us is conceived in the present. The present is the moment in time when we decide what we want to do with our lives. It is never too late to start with the essential things of life; the moment called 'now' is always with us. We must listen anew to the words of the Holy Spirit: "Today if you hear his voice, do not grow stubborn as in those days of rebellion . . ."[45]

The easiest way of coming into the presence of God is to enter through stillness, in anticipation of God's Word. Stillness will enable us to put some distance between ourselves and the events of our everyday lives, our fears, and our desires. It will prevent us from becoming victim to them, and we will always be able to find time for the essentials. Being prepared to take enough time for these essentials is the first sign of a real turning about, an important change of direction, which will result in the necessary inner changes.

"There's never enough time (for this or that)!" is something we frequently hear! If a person is prepared to find the necessary time to observe stillness, they will soon expose this ridiculous pretence for what it is! How can we devote hours to a total absorption in media and not be willing to take the time needed to initiate real and useful changes in our lives and characters? Letting go of the unimportant things during our Prayer of Stillness helps us to muster up the courage we need before we can redefine our use of time and get our priorities right.

How can we make time for the Prayer of Stillness in our daily routine? It is best for beginners to start with fifteen to thirty minutes and then to gradually increase the time allowed. If we never seem to have enough time first thing in the morning, we should perhaps start going to bed in good time so that we will be able to get up earlier. Deciding to put an end to our lethargy on that one point leads to a decisive turn of events. Our willingness to spend sufficient time seeking fellowship with God every day is in itself a sign of our devotion.

As is the lot of all pastors, it has often fallen to me to minister to dying parishioners. Many of those dying appeared to have understood, after they had reached a certain degree of self-denial, what it meant to use their time purposefully. They were filled with creative powers, not only that, they also knew how to put those powers to good use. Others, unfortunately the majority, wasted their time without such realisation and so failed to attain life's most important goals.

The main obstacle to my own spiritual progress was that I found that I was unable to remain in quietude and stillness before God for any great length of time. Consequently, some years ago, I decided that in order to put an end to my particular brand of spiritual lethargy, I would devote half of my weekly day off to meditation and inner stillness. I spent the allotted time each week in silent meditation until I felt that I was able to be still and that all inner resistance had broken down. It took me several weeks to arrive at my goal. Since then, I have learnt to consider the time I spend in inner stillness as an absolute necessity—as an act which makes me able to walk my path with God—and not as just a sheer waste of time.

Our 'time' is a gift from God and a sign of his patience. Wilfrid Stinissen is right when he states that "God did not create us to automatically answer with 'Yes'. What would love be worth if that were the case? He wants us to decide of our own free will what our answer will be. He is waiting for our 'Yes'. 'Time' itself is the extent and the length of his waiting. God asks us, 'Do you want to . . . ?' and then he gives us the 'time' needed for our 'Yes' to mature . . . 'Here I stand knocking at the door . . .' [46] The fact that he is standing at the door and waiting is what constitutes time . . . His giving us time shows us just how much he values our answer."[47]

Food for thought:
– What takes up most of your time and energy?
– Are you able to get back to the important things when you have lost
  yourself in distractions?

– How much time do you take daily to be alone with God?
– How much time are you willing to put aside for an encounter with God?

Arise, Shine; for Thy Light Is Come!

The main point here is that we are to 'arise', which means 'to get up (especially from the dead) and present oneself'—compare with Ephesians 5: 14 (page 18)—The mediaeval preacher, John Tauler, emphasised the necessity of such an arising in his sermon on Isaiah 60: 1. He tries to make his listeners see the importance of 'enlightenment'.

"Man must do his part and rise from everything that is not God, away from himself and all created things. And as he rises, the depth of his soul is seized by a powerful longing to be denuded and freed from everything that separates it from God. And the more he leaves behind all that is finite, the stronger his longing grows. It transcends itself, and when this denuded ground is touched, the desire often overflows into flesh and blood and bone. People react differently when touched by this desire. Some approach it with natural reason, with images borrowed from it, and with high speculations. Thus, they bring confusion to this depth. They stifle the desire by trying to understand what is happening to their souls. They derive a certain peace from their efforts, but it is an illusory peace . . . Some of them follow their own ideas and choose their own techniques in prayer and meditation, or perhaps imitate what other people are doing. They believe that in this way, they are preparing the ground of their souls, and they expect to find peace . . . But, alas, it is a false peace . . . On the other hand, we encounter noble souls so steeped in truth that it shines forth in them. They permit God to prepare the ground, leaving themselves entirely to him. By this act of self-surrender, they refuse to cling to anything of their own, be it their works, their special devotions, what they undertake, and what they leave aside. They accept all things from God in humble awe and refer them back

to him in total detachment, bowing lowly to the divine will. Whatever God may send, they are well-pleased to accept it. Peace or strife are all one to them."[48]

True peace is only to be found in Christ and in our own selves. What Tauler exposes here is nothing but our vain attempts to find such inward peace elsewhere. The Lord Jesus always extolled self-denial as the best route to happiness. It is not the aspect of stillness as such which helps us to find inward peace; it is Jesus himself! The peace promised by the writers of the Gospels is not derived from a 'special kind of feeling' which comes over us when we intentionally let go of distracting thoughts. It is the fruit of an inner attitude a fruit which has its roots in reconciliation between God and mankind.

Countless numbers of people long for inner peace; they long for what they call 'peace of mind'. They are not necessarily aware of having done anything terribly wrong, nevertheless, they are badly affected by a negative disposition. Being discontented with their lot in life (some call it 'fate') makes them depressed, and they become prone to gloomy moods. This will often lead to secret addictions, and they become enslaved, trapped. None of us will enter peace until our lives and our innermost convictions are in line with God's will. Getting to the place where we are in agreement with God's will means going through several phases, none of which can be overlooked. Mother Theresa describes these phases in a most plausible way:

The fruit of silence is prayer,
the fruit of prayer is faith,
the fruit of faith is love,
the fruit of love is service,
the fruit of service is peace.

While we are reaching out for this much sought-after peace, we should expect the eagerness with which we willingly surrender our lives to Christ to grow accordingly. We should counter every little lack, every absence of peace, with a desire to come closer to God. "They have to abandon their presumptions and arrogant ways and begin the strenuous work of self-denial, following the steps of Our Lord Jesus Christ in humility and love. By dying to self they have to learn what it means to truly arise."[49] Tauler speaks deliberately of the necessity of learning to let go at heart, deep down in our innermost souls, where our concession has given God the right to enter, and the right to change us; change our hearts and our lives. We must be willing to search our own souls and the Prayer of Stillness lends us the necessary willingness.

What causes the transformation? Is it our own self-denial or God's Holy Spirit? Or, more to the point, would the Holy Spirit possibly be able to change us and use us if we were not first willing to deny ourselves? Both elements are indispensable; discipleship without the preparedness to take up our cross and allow God to do his works in us is unthinkable. We would have a distorted concept of God if we believed that our lives could prove to be good or acceptable without our having to 'Carry our Cross'; self-sacrificing self-denial was the path that even the Lord Jesus had to tread before anything could be accomplished.[50]

Food for thought:
– *To what extent do you think you are able to search your own soul? Will you be able to make the necessary decisions when the time comes?*
– *What do you imagine it will be like when you awaken and arise? Are you prepared to start now?*

Being God's Child

Being the spiritual child of a spiritual father—a child of God—is a thing very peculiar to the Christian faith; it is an aspect which is not to be found in other religions. Quietude is where we are confronted with our innermost selves. We meet face to face with our own motives, and so it is in the Prayer of Stillness that we meet Christ who has promised us that he will, through his Holy Spirit, "come to us and make his dwelling with us"[51], the moment we freely decide to live our lives in obedience to him.

Klaus Berger describes this process as follows: "Under the covenant of the New Testament God creates children for himself out of mere humans, at the same time creating a close and intimate relationship; a relationship modelled on the closeness of parents to their children. No relationship can be closer; a person cannot become more alike to God than they can by being chosen, or by being called to be his child."[52]

The Lord Jesus uses the word 'child' in this context several times to show that our faith in him begins when we become aware of how totally helpless we are. When we admit to our own forlorn state, we will see that we are far removed from the state in which God expects us to find us. Therefore, we must speak of sin. We soon discover that not even our greatest efforts can bring us up to God's standards. We dare not deny the cause of mankind's separation from God or the fact that the cause must be overcome if we wish to speak of God's acceptance of us and call ourselves God's children. The Prayer of Stillness will help us to reach the point where self-knowledge and awareness drives us towards the Lord Jesus and towards dependency on him alone, not allowing us to lose our way amongst lame excuses and condemnations. This is where we begin to rob our ego of its dominance, where we stop allowing it to get in our way!

These may be quite familiar words to us, but the absolute necessity of making a personal decision to obey Christ is very often either not mentioned at all, or it is looked at in the utmost sceptical manner. Such an attitude is not in the least bit evangelical—that is in the way that the writers of the Gospels (the 'Evangelists' in the true and original meaning of the word) meant it to be—quite apart from being unfounded. We must remember that accepting Jesus in just this way is an indispensable condition, without which there is no hope of entering the Kingdom of Heaven.

Whenever the wish to become a child of God is awakened in a person's heart, something special happens: "God is able to choose those who have come thus far, for such a person has set aside all that is haughtiness and conceit; they can rightly assess the situation between God and themselves; they no longer have any delusions about their own relative grandeur."[53] Bernard de Clairvaux emphasised that although it is God's will that all people should be saved, salvation can only be attained by those who want it, and who give their consent. God would never give a person the precious gift of his salvation, "... before making sure that they really want it."[54] God does not force anyone to come to him, but as soon as a person "... begins to have just a fragmentary passion for him, God draws that person to himself."[55] That person accepts forgiveness from God, then turns towards Christ, and the transformation begins.

A crucial factor is our own awareness of what has happened; we have a new parentage; we are God's children. It was not for nothing that the tempter tried to undermine Jesus's conception of himself as God's son. Two of the temptations in the wilderness began with the words: "If you are the Son of God . . ."[56] The evil one knew that Jesus would become vulnerable in every respect if he could be made to give up the awareness of his parentage.

The same thing happens to us. Even a very strong-willed person will eventually capitulate to the very subtle kind of temptation which always attacks us at our weakest spot. The only way of putting up any kind of effective resistance against temptation is by being aware that we are 'a child of God'. Paul expresses this clearly when he writes about the inner struggles of Christians: "For all who are moved by the Spirit of God are sons of God. The Spirit you have received is not a spirit of slavery leading you back into a life of fear, but a Spirit that makes us sons, enabling us to cry 'Abba! Father!' In that cry the Spirit of God joins with our spirit in testifying that we are God's children; and if children, then heirs."[57]

Within the context of this deliberately wished-for dependency, God now gives us a resolute will to do what is good and acceptable, and not only that, it is him working in us that makes us able to do the deeds of his own chosen purpose.[58] Our will is fused with God's will to bear fruit, and the fruit of that fusion will be the much sought-after peace!

Food for thought:
– *How do you know for sure that you are a child of God? What personal experience can you identify with this certainty?*
– *Does this certainty bring you joy? Does it help you through your day-to-day life?*

Returning to the Heart

The word 'heart', in a Biblical sense, means the 'centre or inner-most part of a person'. Our lives radiate from this centre, whether we wish to believe it or not! The culture in which we live, being for the most part intellectual and therefore steered by the 'head' or mind, tends to neglect the fact that the 'heart' is the true hub of life. It is the place " . . . from which we can speak the words 'I' or 'thou'; it is the centre of a person."[59] It is inevitable that as we enter the Prayer of Stillness, from the moment we decide to stop the conscious flow of our thoughts, be it for only a limited amount of time, our attention will be drawn to this centre in such a way as to make us intuitively know that our thoughts are in fact guided by our hearts. Whatever thoughts insist on surfacing from the inner stillness will reveal the true state of our hearts. Our thoughts are what make us what we are, even if we are reluctant to accept this as a reality. We would be shocked to the core and would see ourselves in quite a different light if we admitted that such strange and often unpleasant thoughts were a true reflection of our innermost being.

Contemplative prayer was already known as 'the prayer from the heart' in early times, and the monks of the eastern world understood it to be a form of 'inner composure'. It meant letting go of all distractions, linked at the same time with calling upon the name of the Lord Jesus and quoting or reading Bible verses aloud. These monks were convinced that in so doing they could be sure that God would take up his dwelling in their hearts.[60]

The stillness, in which we allow ourselves to be drawn more and more to Jesus, will lead us to a deeper knowledge of ourselves and away from any hint of hypocritical self-sufficiency—a deeper knowledge which is, at the same time, very closely connected to our increasing knowledge of God.

This explains why in the Bible the heart is considered to be the centre of faith and all that transpires through faith. The heart is also the centre of our own will. It is the place where we can encounter God, and it is simultaneously the place where we can consciously decide to ignore God.

Is it not true that the story of our lives deals mainly with the events and the happenings that our hearts have passed through; the victories it has gained and the defeats which it has suffered? Love and salvation fix the course of our lives, but we dare not forget that unhealed or festering emotional wounds and unsated desires remain highly influential. Whereas love and salvation teach us to trust in God's guidance, the negative traits will bring us under the rule of powers bearing a thousand names. Why are we surprised when these powers lead us to places we would never have dreamed of going to? On numerous occasions, we exclaim: "Oh, but I certainly didn't mean to do that!" Which only goes to show that there are powers which have far more force than our own powers of reasoning. Evil is a reality which must be taken seriously. We are called upon to let go, and in letting go we open our hearts to God's influence.

When God enters a person's heart, he is closer to us than we are to our very selves! S. S. Singh describes this phenomenon most expressively when he says: "Neither by understanding nor by seeing can we find the truth, but only from the depth of our hearts . . . we need no book-learning to see and recognise Christ: we need only to give him our hearts."[61] Singh did not wish to limit the influence or the power of the Holy Scriptures; he merely wanted to point out that great Biblical knowledge is of little use if the Word of God is not accepted in the heart. Recovering Biblical spirituality goes hand in hand with rediscovering our own heart and its spiritual, rather than physical, function.

Food for thought:
– How much attention do you pay to the thoughts of your heart?
– How far do you go in your efforts to satisfy the justifiable or legitimate
  desires of your heart?

Seeking God Only

As we grow more able to enter into stillness by way of prayer, we will also become more and more able to see clearly exactly who God in Christ is and what he means to us. The person praying may still tend to confuse the 'thou', who is God, with the 'I', who is their own self. They may mistake impressions or visions born of their own feelings for the voice of God. The Prayer of Stillness will help us along this path paved with self-knowledge, and it will help us to distinguish between our own feelings and the 'thou' we are reaching out for. During the stillness we keep our emotions at bay and turn towards the 'thou' who is Jesus. When this happens, the meditant feels a pronounced urge to hear and act upon the Word of God. At times, when distractions or egocentricity take control of us, this special kind of stillness—where we rest afloat and allow our yearning for God and his Word to carry us with the current—will help us to find our way back to him who loves us.

That meditants might also receive impressions and/or inspirations which will leave them disconcerted is a possibility that cannot be ruled out. They should be warned against attempting to attract such experiences to themselves through their own efforts, no matter in what way such experiences appear to be interesting or spiritual. Really important inspirations will be repeated in some form or other, and so it is advisable to just let go of such 'impressions'. Most mystics think that it is advisable to ignore unusual revelations and visions. Richard of Saint Viktor states that ". . . (just) as Christ attested his transfiguration by the presence of Moses and Elias, so visions should not be believed unless they have the authority of Scripture."[62]

Listen to what Sadhu Sundar Singh says about what we should expect of God when we pray: "The essence of prayer does not lie in our wanting something from God, but in our opening our hearts to him . . . praying is not asking; it is rather more the unification of ourselves and God . . . praying is not an effort to wring from God the things that we need. Praying is a desire to know God and to have the presence of God, creator of all things, within us."[63]

Whether what we experience in prayer is unfeigned or not can be judged by the obedience to Christ and the ministry to others which a genuine experience will propagate. We will see that, in contrast to eastern religions, the Christian faith revolves around a 'thou-I' relationship as the centre point of prayer. Being based on a 'father and child' relationship is what makes our faith absolutely unique in this respect.

At this stage we must differentiate quite clearly between the state entered into by meditants practising the Prayer of Stillness and the type of mysticism which claims that God is present in *all* human beings. The Prayer of Stillness requires that meditants make a conscious decision to seek fellowship with God. Only after making this choice do they begin to take part in a living dialogue with God through his Son Jesus Christ. It is easy to mistake the one kind of mysticism for the other, particularly when we allow ourselves to be guided by our emotions, by images, opinions, and thoughts, rather than by Jesus Christ in person and by his Word. Are we not then, in succumbing to such temptation, disobeying the Second Commandment, which forbids the making of carved images and likenesses?

The Prayer of Stillness aims to lead us away from all false images. When we let go, we will see the Image of God as revealed in Christ, who was crucified and who rose again from the dead. At this point we must mention a common misconception about the meaning of the sacraments. If sacraments, such as baptism or the Eucharist, are thought of as a substitute for personal decisions made by the believer—thereby making such decisions superfluous—then the meditant will be running the risk of encountering some kind of 'second I' rather than the 'thou' who is God as revealed in Christ. Only by consciously concentrating on Christ and his Word can we be saved from deviation. We are not, or should not be, attempting to experience Christ subjectively, as if through some kind of procedure or technique. Our tendency to hold fast to our own imagined picture of God, or to some traditional picture which has been handed down from generation to generation will, sooner or later, lead to disappointment. This tendency to visualise God as we wish him to be shows quite plainly that we are still trying to escape the necessity of making the personal commitment to obey Christ completely. Let us all be warned against every kind of 'Feel-Good Faith', which instead of aspiring to obedience, merely brings about a certain sense of emotional satisfaction and pleasing experiences. This kind of faith has nothing to offer in the way of lasting consolation, comfort, or hope.

Many a meditant will one day realise that they believe in God (and in his Word): "for their own sake rather than for God's sake. Having realised, they will then begin to think about their relationship to God and will, eventually, begin to love God for his own sake rather than their own."[64] This particular kind of conundrum is not usually uncovered without prayer.

As we progress down this path towards awareness, it is important not to get stuck along the way. If we do, we will have to swallow the same kind of critical remarks as God directed at the Israelites: "When you fasted and lamented . . . was it indeed in my honour that you fasted?"[65] There is no righteousness in doing what is morally right and acceptable, i.e. 'good', merely for the sake of good in itself as opposed to evil. If we are not motivated by a selfless love and a wish to do good for God's sake, we will fail to attain our goal.

We imagine that we 'know' God, but our supposed knowledge of him is often based upon (the very shaky grounds of) what we know about him, instead of on his Word and on what we have experienced through faith in him and with him. The time we spend in the quietude of the Prayer of Stillness is meant to help us leave the first state behind us and enter into the second. We should not be content just to hear words from Scripture or to learn verses by heart; we must long to surrender ourselves to the person who is Jesus Christ and who is behind those words. The Spanish mystic Miguel de Molinos stated quite correctly: "The soul does not become mature through much talking, and much pondering over God, but by loving much. We must attain this love by way of perfected self-denial and inner stillness. All these things are the works of God's love."[66] Most of life's problems can only be resolved in the light of an encounter with God, who is waiting for us to requite his love. The place where this takes place is not in the 'head' but in the 'heart'. The heart is the centre, and from that centre we can view life without erring.

Food for thought:
– *When do you feel that you are really close to God? When do you sense that his Word is really speaking to you?*
– *What do you do to make this happen?*

*"It is by accepting your presence in everything
that I shall become what you wish me to be."*[67]
Jean Pierre de Caussade

Part Three

Practical Information, Instructions, and Advice

Learning a Lesson from the Beggars

An Indian bears witness:

*Despite the fact that I had often known difficulties and great need in
my own life, as a sincere supporter of the Communist Party, I had always
been concerned about the general well-being of the underprivileged sec-
tions of society.*

*One day I went to Kalighat, a place where an especially large number of
beggars live. I wanted to talk to the beggars and find out more about their
way of life. I was hoping that I would be able to do something or other
to help them. When I arrived, I discovered that the people there were not
at all, like what I had imagined them to be. I was curious to know more
about them, and they asked me to come back the next day. The next day,
I noticed that a relief organisation was ministering among the beggars
and looking after them. These people told me about God and introduced
the Bible to me. I felt the immediate need to put the whole of my past life
in order. One day, my new friends from the Bartimaeus Project gave me
a booklet called 'The Prayer of Stillness'. I immediately started trying to
practice what the booklet said every day. Praying in this special way has
led me to a joyful life lived in faith.*

Snehangshu Molia, Kolkata

The ideal surrounding for our Prayer of Stillness would be a place
with something of the atmosphere of the wilderness about it—a

place similar to the one that Jesus chose—a place where we are robbed of every creature comfort and where the distractions of the town can no longer offer us a hiding place.

1. The Prayer of Surrender

Begin with a prayer surrendering yourself completely to Christ; make a clear declaration of your intention, saying that you are going to let go of everything which might hinder you and keep you from following Christ. You may like to repeat the following prayer, formulated by Brother Klaus:

My Lord and my God,
take everything from me
that keeps me from thee.

My Lord and my God,
give everything to me
that brings me near to thee.

My Lord and my God,
take me away from myself
and give me completely to thee.

The name of Jesus may be substituted quite easily for the name of God. This prayer of surrender and dedication is of great importance because in it you declare your intention, i.e. the main reason for entering into stillness. Declaring that intention will automatically keep any distractions within certain bounds. Consequently, you should remain aware of the initial intention throughout the prayer. Make a conscious decision to be still right at the start; a short prayer will be helpful, for example: "At this present moment I let go of all distracting thoughts, fears, memories, and feelings. I am here for you (thee) only, just as you are (thou art) here for me. You gave (Thou gavest) up everything for us, that we might be saved. I give up everything to live only for you (thee) and to grow in your (thy) likeness.'

2. Meditating on the Scriptures

It is useful, at the beginning, alongside the prayer of surrender, to read a few Bible verses. It is best to ponder carefully over the chosen passage, leaving your Bible open in front of you. Referring to works such as 'Meditations on the Gospel According to Luke' by Karin Johne can also be of great help. The primary objective at this stage is to assume (i.e. take on) an open awareness and a receptive attitude which will enable you to find out what God is saying to you and to understand how he wants to change your life through his Gospel. Pray your way through the passage; that is speak to Christ about his Word and wait for his answer. The stillness around and in you will help you to hear the Word of God and will draw you closer to Christ. At this point we must emphasise that any changes the meditant experiences are solely the work of the Holy Spirit of God, and must not on any account be ascribed to a particular method or technique.

3. Inner Composure

Try to find a quite place where you can get away from the noise and hectic schedule of daily life. Do not, however, allow yourself to become agitated if it is not possible to escape noise from 'the world outside'. Always choose a time when your senses are fully awake.

Make sure that you are sitting or kneeling comfortably either on a chair or on a prayer stool. Be sure to avoid any cramped position or hunched shoulders; correct posture is essential and will keep distraction at bay. Bad posture can considerably hinder any kind of meditation. This is only common sense; physical discomfort always causes our thoughts to wander!

Choose a word: Choose a word as a symbol of your intention, which is to enter God's presence. This very intention gives the chosen *word* a 'holy' character; the *word* is 'holy' because of the way you intend to use it. Your chosen *word* expresses your desire to enter God's presence and to submit yourself to his will. Ask the Holy Spirit to help you find a suitable *word*, for example; *'Lord', 'Jesus', 'Father', 'Love', 'Peace', 'Shalom', 'Grace'* . . . your *word* should be one which you are familiar with; it should be as simple as possible, and it should not have more than two syllables. It should signify your intention—that of inwardly moving towards God. Do not suddenly change the *word* at any time during your period of meditation, as changing the *word* would distract you from the stillness.

Be still, quiet, and calm: This stillness is the centre; the very heart of the prayer. It means opening the whole of your heart and your spirit to Christ. Close your eyes so that your thoughts will not be distracted by what you can see! Linger before God in stillness; be prepared to receive whatever it is that he may want to give you. You will find that after about thirty seconds of stillness and quietude a new thought will drift into your mind, but do not be alarmed.

Each time a new thought wanders into your mind, concentrate on your *word*. Repeating your *word* softly, in an undertone, will help you to let go of the distracting thought; it will help you to leave your worries and anxieties behind you. Keep on banishing all unwanted thoughts in this way until you are inwardly open to Christ.

Take no notice of your breathing: Our breathing is normally shallow and regular. During the Prayer of Stillness, we pay no particular attention to our breathing. Quite the opposite is true of eastern forms of meditation, which usually consider breathing to be of great importance.

Do not try to achieve anything in or through your stillness. You should be seeking Christ's presence, striving to be moulded in his likeness by letting go of everything else, just as he did. The pleasant feeling of achievement, which comes after a successfully completed exercise, is nothing when compared to the growing inner readiness and the eagerness to serve God. We dare not forget that even while we are letting go, Christ crucified continues to be our example. As long as we hold fast to that one idea, God's love will be revealed to us time after time. God's love is accessible only through an ever-increasing identification with Christ crucified. We will find that letting go helps us to identify with Christ.

How can we cope with thoughts that are not so easily banished and thoughts that are hindering progress because they surface again and again? You should behave, as far as possible, in the following manner: If certain thoughts are making you aware of incorrect conduct or impure character traits, then sincerely ask for forgiveness from the very bottom of your heart. Speak just three or four words, for example: "Lord! Forgive me!" On no account should you try to discuss your transgressions with God. Open your inner self—your heart—to God's mercy and to his grace. It is only through his grace and his Holy Spirit that you have access to God's presence.

Are you repeatedly plagued and tormented by the same or similar thoughts and fears, although you are quite aware that they are hindering your progress? Consciously choose to detach yourself from them by saying a short prayer. For example, if a particular person's actions or words are a frequent source of pain to you, say a short prayer such as: "Lord, I lay the pain beneath your cross!" Do not try to carry on a discussion with God about your suffering!

As you become more and more accustomed to being 'still' before God, your prayers will grow more and more earnest and sincere. The sudden need to pour out cascades of words and vain repetitions, which is in reality a subconscious attempt to make God hear, and above all answer your prayers, will be replaced by an inner certainty; you will know that God is there and that he will hear you. Faith and an objective obedience are far more important than "making many words."[68] The same principle applies to intercession, which is the final stage of our prayer.

We must not forget that having once let go of depressing thoughts does not in itself guarantee that they will not be back! The initial act of letting go does not prevent such thoughts from returning. What we need most is a growing awareness of having detached ourselves from such thoughts, coupled with a new and profound manifestation of God's love for us and for our lives. You will have to be patient. Meditants who feel that they are not making any progress may need to consult a pastor.

4. Worship

Encountering God's absolute *holiness* will awaken a spontaneous yearning deep within us to *worship him*. This stage of our prayer is often called 'contemplation'.

We see that the word '*contemplation*' contains the Old English word '*templ*', which means 'a consecrated space or place in the presence of God used for worship'. We aim, by means of the Prayer of Stillness, to transform our inward lives into a place where Christ is not only encountered but also worshipped.

5. Re-read the Bible verses that you read at the start

6. Intercession

Intercede for others; making requests on their behalf and bringing them before God. Intercession will become easier as time passes, and meditants will no longer experience any difficulty in spending a considerable amount of time praying for others. They will learn how to pray without unnecessary repetitions and will pray with a steadfast determination presenting their petitions before God with a certain simplicity.

How much time should your Prayer of Stillness take? Most people need twenty to thirty minutes before they arrive at a state of inner quiet and calm. The length of time needed should normally be within certain predetermined limits. Each individual will discover with experience just how much time they will need to put aside. If possible, you should take time for two such periods of prayer a day. Early morning and afternoon are the best times to choose. Utter surrender is of much more importance than the amount of time you spend in prayer, but it is quite possible that the extent to which you surrender yourself to God may be closely connected with how willing you are to spend time with God. We can only wish that every meditant will one day discover that God himself is longing to enter into the very closest form of fellowship with us, because he created us and loves us. Whenever possible you should put aside plenty of time for these daily encounters with God, they are linked to what Jesus promised: ". . . and your Father who sees what is secret will reward you."[69]

We are not replacing other forms of prayer. In fact, we will find that we are able to pray more intensely than before. If you will just try this 'new' form of prayer, you will see how the Prayer of Stillness gradually takes effect in your life, and the fruits of this particular form of prayer will soon become noticeable. They will be more easily recognisable in your day-to-day life than in the actual times of prayer.

Food for thought:
– *Are you prepared to put aside at least half an hour for each period of prayer?*
– *Ask yourself what time of day you will best be able to take time for God: mornings or evenings? It will be better if you are able to take time for the Prayer of Stillness twice a day.*

The following figures show which positions are especially suitable for the Prayer of Stilless:

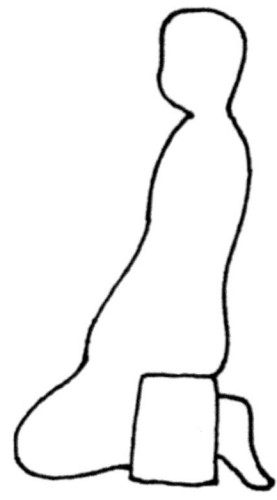

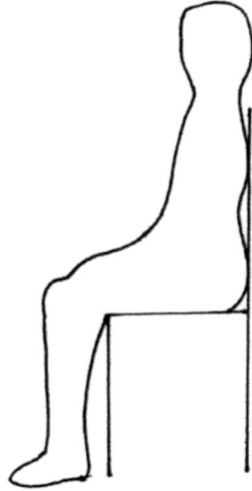

Kneeling on a low stool
or on a special prayer stool

Sitting on an upright chair

*"A practical Christian must above all be one who practises
the perpetual return of the soul into the inner sanctuary."*
Thomas Kelly

Part Four

God Is All Around Us

A Child Begins to Meditate

An Indian bears witness:

*I work as a social worker in Rabindra Sarani, a district of Kolkata. I go to
see the beggars there every day. When we were given the booklet called 'The
Prayer of Stillness', I began to hand it out among the groups of beggars, and
we started to meditate on what it told us. I also explained what the booklet
said to those who could not read. This was of great benefit to me, and it was
very useful in my own personal life. I also discovered that the people in my
group were spending more and more time in prayer. I was very pleased about
it because I could see that God was leading and guiding them. One day Mrs
Sonal's son came to me; he was crying. I was surprised and I asked him why
he was crying. He told me that he had secretly read the booklet about 'The
Prayer of Stillness' and that he had found and encountered God through
meditation. The boy is now, to his mother's joy, a totally changed child.*
Sangeeta, Kolkata

Daily Practice; The Need for Inner Composure

The newly acquired awareness needs to be anchored in our inner
soul. The only way of making sure that it is rooted deeply is by daily
practice. Thus, the outward form of the Prayer of Stillness should

not be changed; the same 'method' should be used for as long as possible. The continuity and the duration of daily practice will ensure that the prayer has the delicate equilibrium which it needs to make it a success. You should not expect your personal problems to disappear suddenly; there is no guarantee of immediate results! It is far more important to build a reservoir of deep faith and trust and a growing sense of being dependent upon God alone. A feeling founded on your great love for God and his Word.

Learning to Depend upon the Grace of God Only

When we become more accomplished in the Prayer of Stillness, we will usually begin to notice which things exert the most influence on our lives. We will suddenly recognise that all thoughts which have anything to do with hate, envy, bitterness, immorality, and the like[70] have an extremely disturbing effect on our progress. It makes no difference how insignificant these thoughts may be in themselves—they will exert a significant influence. Even though we might previously have considered such thoughts to be quite normal and had probably learnt to take them for granted, we now discover their power to destroy. Just imagine for a moment that our family, our friends, or even strangers could read such thoughts! Would we not then do anything we could to stop those thoughts? If we cannot answer for our thoughts before other people, how will we ever manage to answer for them before God, who sees everything? The Prayer of Stillness is the place where we become more and more aware of the presence of Jesus Christ, the Lord. This does not necessarily keep us safe from temptation, but it gives us the strength to overcome it.

When all is said and done, it is neither a special form of meditation or prayer, nor is it our knowledge of the Bible. It is not our own good will, nor our very firmest resolutions which will secure for us the much longed-for freedom and bring peace to our souls. God's redeeming and saving arm[71] can *only* be moved by the love which ties us to Christ and the act of surrendering ourselves unto him in contemplative prayer. It is of vital importance that meditants know that they must lay all their shortcomings and their blemishes bare before God the very moment they become aware of them. We will be able to tell just how far we have progressed along the path towards change by the very fact that we begin to ask for forgiveness; an act that renders us truly dependent upon his Grace.

A Change in Disposition

The presence of Christ in our lives will be most noticeable in our disposition or temperament. Each individual person has their own particular disposition, be it positive or negative. Childhood and present situations or surroundings are partly responsible for the natural qualities of a person's character. The person concerned may not even have contributed anything specific towards their disposition, and it is often very difficult to explain how certain character traits have been acquired. The fact remains that a great deal depends on our disposition; a positive disposition will usually make us capable of the most wonderful achievements, whereas a negative disposition will hold us back and often exercise a destructive power over us, playing havoc and making life hard to bear. A tendency towards obsessive or addictive behaviour is in many cases the result of a negative disposition.

In principle, we should all be able to improve our way of life, provided we are willing to undertake certain steps. The problem is that having gained self-awareness and an insight into how we function in no way guarantees that we will be able to use that knowledge in a practical way. The Prayer of Stillness puts us through a process whereby we draw closer and closer to Christ. It is the path leading us to fulfilment in Christ, enabling us to live out the word of Paul: "...

be always joyful; pray continually, give thanks whatever happens; for this is what God in Christ wills for you."[72] The process enables us to put our new awareness into action. In the stillness of our prayer, it is God himself who is asking us to let him make whatever changes are needed. We cannot tell how long the process will take, but we can be quite certain that God knows, and that he took that time into account when he wrote all our days in his book.[73]

The peace which we have been longing for, and which plays such a crucial role in determining our disposition, is brought about by a harmony between the extent to which we are dependent upon God's grace and our own willingness to lead a life which is holy and free from affections; always prepared to serve God. If this equilibrium is disturbed, our inward peace vanishes and does not return until we have taken all the steps required to re-establish it. Our disposition determines, to a great extent, our lives—even a good night's sleep is a matter of disposition—research has shown that people who suffer from chronic sleeping disorders are often those who feel a desperate need for the love and acknowledgement of their fellow beings and whose whole existence revolves around how others judge them.

The following schema shows the three essential components of inward peace

Dependence upon God's grace and fellowship with Christ crucified

The ability to lead a holy life; free from affections

The willingness and ability to put God's will into action. Vision: clarity of thought and purpose

66

Food for thought:
- *Is your disposition positive or negative? Have you noticed anything that holds you back?*
- *Have you ever noticed whether you are beset by addictive behaviour when you are in a particular mood?*
- *Would you like to change your disposition? For example, would you like to have a more positive disposition?*

Gaining Vision: Clarity of Thought and Purpose

In our time of stillness, our only wish should be to open ourselves intentionally to Christ and his Word, and we need achieve nothing other than this one goal. We will probably never be able to cut off the flow of conscious thought completely, but we can make it take a deliberately chosen and more promising course. By departing from all our 'normal' patterns of thought, as meditants we can create an 'unfilled space' and an 'opening' simultaneously. It is important to recognise that there is a subtle difference between this 'unfilled space' and what Christ called 'empty', meaning 'unoccupied'[74]; Our newly acquired inner composure speaks a silent invitation to Christ; asking him to come and fill the space which has now been made available, and to make all the necessary changes in our characters and lives through his Word and his Holy Spirit. At that same moment the meditant begins to clear a space for a new vision; for a certain sagacity, which will gradually help each individual to recognise their own purpose in life, to discover what they feel they would be best at.

We are told that long before we decided to live our lives for God, he had decided which good deeds we would do for him! ". . . For we are God's handiwork, created in Jesus Christ to devote ourselves to the good deeds for which God has designed us."[75]

When we stumble across these predetermined deeds, we feel like a child at Christmas time who has finally been allowed to unwrap the presents! We are overjoyed when we notice that there are skills and abilities lying dormant in us, literally waiting to be developed and used. We suddenly see new spheres and new opportunities opening before us. Do you still enjoy opening presents? There are so many exciting possibilities hidden in our lives, all of them are marvellous presents and should be opened without delay.

Now we can understand why young people and children should be taught the Prayer of Stillness; only then will they be shown what God has prepared for them. The younger we are when we begin to say "Yes" to God's ways, the more willing we will be to open ourselves to his will.

One of the greatest aims is to let the love for these deeds grow and mature within the bounds of God's plan. Listen to what Sadhu Sundar Singh has to say about God's plan: "There are people who pray as if we could change God's plan. ... We cannot change God's plan, but in prayer we can learn to recognise his plan for us. If we choose a quiet and secluded place to pray, God will speak to us in the language of the heart. ... As soon as God's plans become known to us, we do not seek to change them, but we wish to be in agreement with them. If we learn to understand God's plans through prayer, he will give us the strength to be unison with his will. ... God's plans work for our good and for the good of our neighbours and fellow beings." [76](See also Rom. 8: 28.)

Our new vision will, because it represents a newly defined purpose in our lives, always allow us to use our time to the best advantage. Those who receive a vision, and who are prepared to pay the necessary price for turning their vision into reality, will certainly do everything they can to see their goals fulfilled. "He (God) will finish and make perfect by his grace what you have begun in yourself, he will become a pillar of fire to guide you if you are prepared to follow him uncondi-tionally wherever he leads you."[77] A great many visions need complete dedication, sometimes even a lifelong dedication is needed before the vision becomes a reality. The list bearing the names of those who have lived their lives —and sometimes even died—for a God-given vision, a cause or a purpose, is incredibly long. They are the ones who have prospered the Kingdom of God right here on Earth!

We do not have to compete, vision against vision, since every vision is unique and therefore absolutely individual. Visions can be passed on to another person, but we can never force others to take up our own special vision. Each individual vision is especially made to suit one particular person; the main thing is that each person develops their very own vision and their own purpose. A woman might feel that she has received the vision of giving her children the best possible upbringing, while the next meditant will feel impelled to take care of others or to work amongst marginal groups in their society.

Only one thing is absolutely certain: whatever your vision happens to be, all visions will in some way or other make it easier for others to see and understand God's love for mankind; all visions will make his love credible in a practical way. This is in accordance with the words that Christ taught us: "Thy kingdom come. Thy will be done in earth as it is in heaven."[78] A lot of the things which ail our world will be changed for the better as soon as you and I start to live out the purpose which God meant for our lives. God will manifest the goals he has set for mankind and this world much more quickly—and we can rest assured that his goals are those which will prosper his purpose and his cause. It is all too regrettable that there are so few believers who are really burning with enthusiasm and who understand what it is to develop their visions and to share them with others.

Food for thought:
- *Have you ever seriously considered what God's purpose in your life is? Have you ever wondered what task he has allotted you? Are you willing to spend time on this special prayer, willing to seek God's presence, and willing to recognise his will for your life?*
- *Are you prepared to give God the right to change your life and make you ready and able to do the deeds that he has determined for you?*

Part Five

Do We Really Need the Prayer of Stillness in Our Daily Lives?

People whose dearest wish is to come close to God are usually prepared to sacrifice the time needed to see that wish fulfilled, and so they will gladly devote their time to the Prayer of Stillness. God does not want to exclude any of us from close fellowship with him; in fact, he expects all of us to take up his offer! To quote Francisco de Osuna: "If you told me that you cannot fast, that you cannot undertake a pilgrimage, I would believe you. But when you tell me that you are not capable of love, I do not believe you."[79] It is up to us whether or not we want to love God as unconditionally as possible, and it is we who must decide whether we *want to* take the time needed to seek him actively or not.

Can born-again Christians of all denominations practise the Prayer of Stillness? "They threw out the baby with the bath water" is a rather pointed way of describing what happened when the European Reformation of the sixteenth century caused the church to turn its back on all forms of mysticism. This phrase has often been applied, and no doubt there is a grain of truth in it. The Reformers wanted to be sure that the influence of the Holy Scriptures remained unadulterated and to safeguard believers against any kind of mystical experience that would inevitably distract then from the firm belief in the Word alone. Visions, dreams, mystical experiences, and the like could not, under any circumstances, be allowed to detract from the influence of the Holy Scriptures. 'The Prayer of Stillness', as described in this book, aims at making reading and listening to God's Word easier for us. In the past so much emphasis was laid on talking to God that we quite forgot about listening to him. Prayer is the tool which will help us gain access to Christ's presence and to his Word more easily. Learning to be still makes it much easier for us to listen to God's Word, because in the process of stillness we are transformed into the kind of fertile ground in which the seed of the Word can be sown. We do not expect anything to result from the practice of the prayer in itself. What we do believe is that the Holy Spirit of God can change a person's life more effectively if that person matures in inwardness. The Prayer of Stillness can, therefore, be practised by any sincere Christian.

All of those who start out along the path of stillness will invariably feel a certain uneasiness at the beginning. The uneasiness of realising that we do not love God *as well or as much* as we should has a therapeutic value. We suddenly feel a need to find God at any cost. At the top of our list of 'dearest wishes' is the hope that each and every meditant, indeed all mankind, will reach a point where they experience this need to find God.

Should then everyone practice the Prayer of Stillness? There are people who are able to compose themselves for long periods of time. They are able to remain still, reaching out for God and concentrating on his presence without being distracted by their own thoughts. Such a person will be able to manage without the Prayer of Stillness. Those who dwell continually in the place we are striving to reach, those who can enter directly into the presence of God, and those who are always willing and prepared to do his will, have already attained the goal! This book is meant to encourage those who do not have this natural ability and have, as yet, found no other way of breaking through. It was written to help them start out along the path of stillness.

Stop and Think about It!

Do we really have the right to live a life of selfishness, of obsessive desires and sin, a life occupied with plans that only lead us astray, knowing as we do that Jesus Christ died for our shortcomings and inadequacies? Is it right for us to carry on living for the very things which Christ lay down his life to eradicate? Are we to live a life focused only upon our own well-being, although Christ rose again from the dead not only for us, but for all mankind? How can we fear the future and stand trembling before mere humans when he promised us that he holds everything in his keeping? Should we really hold fast to questionable objectives, thoughts, or hopes even though we know that he has given us his liberating Word? Are we shutting ourselves off from the path leading to his love by refusing to let go of our self-love?

Part Six

Attaining the Goal—A Course in Four Stages

Introduction

The following four themes provide a framework on which the contents of this book can be implemented, or grafted, and so take on form in our lives. Each topic quite intentionally stresses a particular point and so makes us more aware of its meaning and importance. The various stages, which are completed in group work, will help us to realise the goal. The Prayer of Stillness, accompanied by any necessary exchange of thoughts or impressions with other members of the group, is an *integral daily part* of the process.

God wants us all to be happy! Most of us will spontaneously agree with this statement, although we are very quick to doubt its validity when happiness hides itself just out of our reach. Sometimes, when we are once again confronted with the suffering and misery of this world, we ask questions which remain unanswered. Despite this, even at times when we might be finding it increasingly difficult to cope with our own lives, we will all gladly agree that God loves us and that he has an individual plan for each and every one of us. We are, in principle, willing to put our trust completely in God, but how are we going to fit this trust into our lives and learn to walk calmly with God towards the future he has for us?[80]

The driving force propelling us towards God is a deeply felt longing, a need which we cannot even identify. This longing may have been increased by our efforts to understand the purpose of life, or it may have been awakened by some specific occurrence in our lives, compelling us to seek God's help. More than just a few of life's difficulties have been brought about by our having become more and more estranged from our fellow-beings, from God, and from our own identities. There comes a moment when we need to recognise our inner longing for God and our desire to be a whole rather than a broken person. When we have recognised our predicament, we will be able to see that this 'longing' must grow and that we must allow it the space to grow in. In fact, the Holy Scriptures describe 'the inner longing for God' as the key to spiritual growth.

The main objectives of this course are as follows:
- to help meditants come closer to themselves and closer to the Lord Jesus Christ.
- to help meditants face up to questions concerning the purpose of their lives.
- that meditants get to know their own hearts and develop the ability to cope with their own emotions, fears, and desires.
- that meditants gain more knowledge of God through encountering Jesus Christ.
- that meditants learn how to *apply* the Word which has been heard.
- that meditants develop a vision for their own lives.

The course consists of four stages, and the participants should work in groups under the leadership of a competent person. If, for whatever reason, this is not possible, individuals can practise the Prayer of Stillness and study the passages of Scripture given for each stage at appropriate intervals. The topics discussed in the course are of a very personal nature, and we have tried to create a warm and friendly atmosphere around the participant.

The topics are the following:
- Getting your Priorities Right
- Daring to Arise and Start Out

– Discovering the Regions of the Heart
– Developing your Own Vision

Stage One
Getting Your Priorities Right

A. What Gives You Your Sense of Self-Esteem?

Many of us do not plan our days very well; we just let time drift by without bothering to think about where it goes. Others manage to create a kind of hectic, day-to-day stress, which can be exciting enough to convince them that they are being useful citizens. The present day motto is, 'The more you do, the more important you are.' Modern-day senior citizens manage to stick to this attitude right through retirement. It is embarrassing for them to have to admit that they are not occupied with anything in particular. Activity gives us a feeling of security and busyness justifies our existence. Anyone who is not in some way creative or productive is a nobody! The result is that we organise our days according to the priorities and activities which we have set for ourselves or, even worse, those which have been set up for us by someone else. We run the risk of having many real needs go unnoticed.

Is our continual busyness merely a camouflage, carefully used to excuse our underlying disinterest in the fundamental questions in life? We assume that 'urgent' things should always be dealt with first. Experience has shown us that it is precisely because there is always something or other which will quickly take on the guise of 'urgency' that we never seem to get around to the things of real importance, which are seldom mentioned and sometimes remain unmentioned for an entire lifetime! The important things are very often put aside to make room for the urgent things. I know numerous people who have never in their whole lives actually attempted to deal with the most fundamental questions in life.

Questions:
– What gives you your sense of self-esteem? Is it the things you achieve?
  Is it your morally impeccable life?
– Is there anything in your life which is stopping you from looking for an
  answer to the fundamental questions in life?

B. Reading and Understanding the Passage

The Dangers of Clinging to Riches: The Story of the Rich Young Ruler

>>16. And now a man came up and asked him, 'Master, what good must I do to gain eternal life?' 17. 'Good?' said Jesus. 'Why do you ask me about that? One alone is good. But if you wish to enter into life, keep the commandments.' 18. 'Which commandments?' he asked. Jesus answered, 'Do not murder; do not commit adultery; do not steal; do not give false evidence; 19. honour your father and mother; (Exod. 20: 12-16.) and love your neighbour as yourself.' (Lev. 19: 18) 20. The young man answered, 'I have kept all these. Where do I still fall short?' 21. Jesus said to him, 'If you wish to go the whole way, go, sell your possessions, and give to the poor, and then you will have riches in heaven; and come and follow me.' 22. When the young man heard this, he went away with a heavy heart; for he was a man of great wealth. 23. Jesus said to His disciples, 'I tell you this: a rich man will find it hard to enter the Kingdom of Heaven. 24. I repeat, it is easier for a camel to pass through the eye of a needle than for a rich man to enter the Kingdom of God.' 25. The disciples were amazed to hear this. 'Then who can be saved?' they asked. 26. Jesus looked at them, and said, 'For men this is impossible; but everything is possible for God.' << (Matt. 19: 16-26, The New English Bible; Oxford/ Cambridge University Press, 1970).

What Does the Passage Tell Us?

This meeting between the Lord Jesus and the Rich Young Ruler tells us that whatever it is which we consciously or unconsciously cleave to, that is what we consider to be our 'riches'. We often refuse to give it up, clinging to it with a remarkable tenacity, and eagerly entering into compromises. The object of our desire may have the outward appearance of being absolutely worthless, but still we cling to it all the more. Even when presented with unmistakable proof of its transience, its utter insignificance, we are still not able to turn away from this false love. Whatever it is that we love becomes suddenly valuable; its value is imparted directly by the love that we heap on it, and thus it infuses all aspects of our lives. The things we cling to most persistently are also those things which very quickly tend to become our graven images, and then we expect them to endow us with happiness.

We can see that the Rich Young Ruler's problem boils down to a matter of where his heart is! Jesus appears to think that it is impossible, from a human point of view, for a person to break free of this situation. The things we love always manage to get and to keep control of us. Even if we do somehow manage to break free of one of these idols, we are running the risk of being enslaved by the next. Wanting to clutch at and cling to anyone or anything—with the exception of God—is something we seem to have in our genes. Our only 'freedom' lies in the freedom of choice; we can choose whom to love and serve! Remember that Jesus said: ". . . for even when a man has more than enough, his wealth does not give him life."[81] In other words, our thirst for life cannot be quenched by transitory things such as worldly goods, but only by God himself. It is easier for a camel to go through the eye of a needle than for us mortals to attain, by means of our own strength and our own achievements, the inward freedom and peace needed to serve God.

Questions:
– What is of especial importance to you? What occupies your thoughts

*and drains you of all energy, leaving you little or no time to deal with
life's real problems and questions?*
*– Do you see any way of changing your situation, any way of letting God
have more room in your life?*

C. What Basic Psychogenic Needs Must Be Satisfied?

Amongst the basic human needs we find; the right to live, love,
and be loved; the need to trust others and achieve some kind of
life's work (i.e. not to have existed for nothing). Bernard de Clairvaux wrote the following: "There are three things for which we
ask in life, and I see no reason why anyone should ask for anything more. Two of those are requests for wealth of a non-material
nature, namely physical and psychological well-being (health for
body and soul). The third is the beatitude, or blessing, of eternal
life. Do not be amazed that I say one should ask God for health
in body and mind; all earthly things are his, just as all spiritual
things are. We should, however, pray more frequently and more
earnestly for our spiritual needs ..."[82]

Needs which have not been satisfied often drive us to obsessions
or addictions if we do not learn how to cope with them. A person
who is forced to deal non-stop with their unfulfilled needs begins
to behave as if they were involved in crisis management and to act
like someone who is constantly struggling to survive. Instead of
achieving contentment, these unfortunate individuals are ceaselessly occupied with satisfying their obsessions.

Questions:
*– Looking at your present situation in life, can you say that your basic
needs are being fulfilled?*
*– Which needs remain unfulfilled? Can you live contentedly knowing that,
or are you suffering deep down inside?*
*– Do you sometimes try to compensate for the lack of fulfilment by indulg-
ing in obsessions or addictions?*

78

D. The Aim of the Prayer of Stillness

We do not put our trust in a particular method as such; instead, we use the Prayer of Stillness as a way of coming closer to God and to ourselves through Christ. As we try to understand the self-denial of Christ crucified, we gradually develop a health-bringing self-denial of our own, enabling us to stand apart from, or even avoid, any situation or circumstance likely to cause us pain or to block our way ahead to Christ. The time spent in stillness is important because during the process of letting go, we experience what Christ meant when he said: "If anyone wishes to be a follower of mine, he must leave himself behind; day after day he must take up his cross and come with me."[83] The mystic John of the Cross tells us that the aim or objective "... does not lie in the diversity or beauty of our thoughts, not in the method employed nor in the various practices or spiritual pleasures, but in the one necessity: In understanding, in true denial of one's self, outwardly and inwardly . . . then nothing but following Christ will help us stride towards the goal."[84]

The Prayer of Stillness helps us to cope with unfulfilled wishes and desires, allowing us to deal successfully with obsessive or addictive behavioural patterns.

Question:
– What does the term 'self-denial' mean to you? Do you understand how self-denial, in the sense that Jesus Christ meant it, could be of personal advantage to you?

Stage Two
Daring to Arise and Start out

A. Introduction

Have you ever discovered how exhilarated you feel when you finally manage to conquer your own sluggishness, or manage to overcome a weakness, even in unimportant matters? Our own experience tells us just how much pleasure and satisfaction we get from even a very small victory, even if a certain amount of sacrifice has been necessary. Strangely enough, our euphoric feelings are forgotten almost as soon as the task is completed.

We will need to start afresh over and over again; each new awakening leads us into a deeper devotion to Christ. The last awakening of all will lead us into eternity! This course with its four stages might just be the challenge that was necessary to start you off in the right direction; perhaps it will give you the courage you need to dare to move on to the next awakening.

Merely being prepared to go through the stages leading to change is a sign that you still have enough control over your thoughts and actions—over your so-called 'willpower'—to realise that changes for the better in your life are very much called for. It proves that you are still aware of what is happening to you and around you, and that you still know that God has a plan for your life.

God's love for mankind insists, even demands, that we repent or 'turn back' and change our ways. We are achieving nothing by refusing to hear his call, except that we are running the risk of wasting time and energy and are in danger of forfeiting our salvation. Every step we take towards God fills his heart with joy; we cause him pain when we tarry and remain caught up in our own dreams, our own fears, and fantasies, or in the bitter reproaches, which we hurl at him or at others or ourselves. Many of these things do indeed create a temporary feeling of security, or even of self-righteousness, but they lead us astray from the path towards the freedom which Christ has promised us.

No one who turns away from an addiction, a besetting sin, or from seeking earthly honours need fear being plunged into consequent unhappiness! Encountering God's love, right there where you walk towards Christ who was crucified and on the third day rose from the dead, is where you will find the fullness of life. Let the way of stillness help you along this path.

Question:
- *Try, for one moment, to imagine God as a living person, full of compassion and long-suffering, a person who has long struggled for you.*
- *He has done so many good things. He has kept you safe for so long; only through his love and faithfulness and through your willingness to trust and follow him has this been possible. Do you not see how he is waiting to lead you on, lead you further? God is real and he is alive and much more besides! There are many passages in the Bible which prove that God is very sensitive to each and every move we make; the seps that we take and the ones that we fail to take. Why? Because he has made us in his likeness! He rejoices with all heaven over each step we take in his direction, and he grieves when we refuse his help and his love. What do you think his thoughts about you and your life look like at this very moment?*

B. The Story of the Prodigal Son
>>11. Again He said: 'There was once a man who had two sons; 12. and the younger said to his father, "Father, give me my share of the property." So he divided his estate between them. 13. A few days alter the younger son turned the whole of his share into cash and left home for a distant country, where he squandered it in reckless living. 14. He had spent it all, when a severe famine fell upon that country and he began to feel the pinch. 15. So he went and attached himself to one of the local landowners, who sent him on to his farm to mind the pigs. 16. He would have been glad to fill his belly with the pods that the pigs were eating; and no-one gave him anything. 17. Then he came to his senses and said, "How many of my father's paid servants have more food than they can eat, and here am I, starving to death! 18. I will set off and go to my father and say to him, 'Father, I have sinned, against

God and against you; 19. I am no longer fit to be called your son; treat me as one of your paid servants.' " 20. So he set out for his father's house. But while he was still a long way off his father saw him, and his heart went out to him. He ran to meet him, flung his arms around him, and kissed him. 21. The son said, "Father, I have sinned, against God and against you; I am no longer fit to be called your son." 22. But the father said to his servants, "Quick! Fetch a robe, my best one, and put it on him; put a ring on his finger and shoes on his feet. 23. Bring the fatted calf and kill it, and let us have a feast to celebrate the day. 24. For this son of mine was dead and has come back to life; he was lost and is found." And the festivities began.<< (Luke 15: 11-24, The New English Bible; Oxford/Cambridge University Press, 1970)

What Does the Passage Tell us?

The son valued neither his relationship to his father nor his inheritance because he did not realise what they were worth! It was therefore quite natural that he should want to lead a life as far away from his father's influence as possible. Once having rejected the protection of his father's house, he became solely dependent upon his own resources. When his money ran out, he was no longer able to make his existence bearable by drowning his fears and loneliness in worldly pleasures, and so he sank into a state of deep despair. It is remarkable how far we can fall when we lose all the outward or material things which support us. Finally, he notices that he has no real personal identity—he probably never did have!—and that the image he had of himself was constructed around externals. His desperate situation forces him to take stock of his attitudes and to see the necessity of turning back and changing his ways. A deep longing begins to assert itself and with that longing comes the memory of his father's house. The young man's memories of his father are somewhat distorted, but nevertheless, they seem to be sufficient to arouse a certain amount of trust in his father's goodness and motivate him to return home.

Most of us do not bother to go looking for any kind of deep meaning or purpose in life until we are forced to do so by a decisive happening in our lives that brings us to a turning point. If we are bowed down under some disastrous stroke of fate, everything that kept us upright and seemed so important fades away—at any event, for at least as long as our suffering lasts!—We then suddenly realise how worthless our graven images really are.

Just as the son in the story had to go through a phase of grave social and spiritual need, causing the memory of his father to find its way back into his consciousness, so it is with us; our illusions and our false expectations must first be toppled before we can see the light! Whether or not you are suffering from a stroke of fate at this very moment, or whether you are driven by the need to come closer to God and enter the circle of his love, whatever your motive, what you are feeling is what we call 'a fundamental longing'.

Questions:
– *What can you learn from the Story of the Prodigal Son? Does the story remind you of anything present or past in your own life? If so, what?*
– *Can you pinpoint the situations in your life when you have been able to return to God's love? What helped you most in your decision to turn back?*
– *Have you withdrawn some areas of your life both from God and from the people around you so that you can live your own life as you please without interference, maybe even in secret?*

C. From the Darkness into Light

In one of his sermons, the German mystic John Tauler, asks his audience to image the transition from darkness to light which a person waking from a deep sleep experiences. Here are his words:

"We should awake and set out (towards the goal)—not only in the sense of physically getting up and moving forward step by step, but more importantly in the sense of letting go and freeing ourselves of everything that is not God or of God, even to the extent of letting go of our own selves."

Basically, we are speaking of the 'process of dying' which will lead us to true life, a process which Paul speaks about in his Epistles. On the one hand we are being asked to abandon all the things which might encumber us and prevent us from drawing closer to God; we can do this only through the forgiveness of Christ and the conscious act of letting go. On the other hand we need to develop a close relationship with Christ; we must listen to him and so discover his love for us. The New Testament calls this twofol experience 'faith'.

Self-denial and finding genuine life go hand in hand; God is not prepared to do his works on us and through us to a greater extent than we are prepared to become more and more like Christ. Each really big change will begin with the change that takes place in our hearts. While we go through the process of letting go of everything which has up until now hindered us, we are following Jesus Christ, who by dying went through the valley of the shadow of death and suffered the most incredible loneliness imaginable. "Whosoever will lose his life for my sake."[85] (as Jesus is speaking about himself this really means 'for Jesus Christ's sake'). The person who loves their life for Jesus Christ's sake will never again live for worries and anxieties, for greed, or any such similar thing but will gain true life everlasting!

Questions:
- *Can you imagine that in being free from everything which is stopping you from following Christ, you will find that much longed-for happiness?*
- *Do you believe that as you follow him, more and more of his love will be revealed to you?*

– As you practise the Prayer of Stillness, do you see the very first signs of that freedom?

D. Living with the Inexplicable

In most circumstances we have very little, if any, means of controlling the wounds inflicted upon our soul and they will inevitably affect our frame of mind. We just 'suffer in silence'. There are situations where only God can give us the strength to hold on and to continue along our path with him. The Prayer of Stillness will help you to distance yourself emotionally from the suffering on a day by bay basis. It will help you to keep going under the pressures which such wounds cause. If ". . . even the hairs of your (our) head(s) have all been counted."[86] and ". . . we know that all things work together for good to them that love God,"[87] then God will surly ". . . turn our mourning into gladness."[88] Do you believe that? Giving our lives to Christ and placing ourselves in his hands will help us to believe that he holds and keeps everything in his hands, even if exactly the opposite seems to be true. The social workers who are involved in our work amongst India's beggars are continually telling us how important it is for them to beable to put the misery caused by extreme suffering out of their conscious minds, to create a distance between what they see and what they feel. The daily Prayer of Stillness achieves just that, and they can go about their work caring for the beggars, leaving their burden with God.

Questions:
– Are there things which are causing you pain and suffering at this very moment? Do they drain you of every ounce of energy, so that you are hardly able to devote yourself to anything else, let alone anything new?
– Does the Prayer of Stillness help you to put some distance between yourself and your pain?

E. Give Your Time to God

The decision to spend time with God and to take time daily to foster our own spiritual growth and development is probably one of the most important decisions we can make. Repenting, turning back and starting anew is only possible under the guidance of the Holy Spirit, we need to let him do his works on us.

You should visualise the time spent in stillness as an expression of your desire to surrender yourself totally; in fact, it should become a part of that very surrender. Consider carefully before you make the decision, but when you have made it, stick to it! Do not change your mind continually. Never regret the time you have given to God. Quite the opposite should be the case. Feel encouraged to give him not just your time, but everything!

Have you ever regretted spending time with a person who you love deeply? If you are willing to spend time with God, you are deliberately moving forwards. You are avoiding those thoughts that come creeping into your mind and then try to persuade you that 'everything is pointless anyway', which is what happens if God does not fill the aching emptiness inside us. There is no substitute for close fellowship with God; neither an intellectual faith nor religious experiences of any kind can fill the gap. The Holy Scriptures warn us again and again to beware of being lulled into a false sense of security.

Questions:
– *Are you prepared to sacrifice the time needed to be still before God?*
– *Have you been able to find the time every day for the Prayer of Stillness, since you started?*
– *Is it easy to find the time, or do you come up against all sorts of apparently insurmountable obstacles? If so, what are those obstacles?*

F. Learning to Put a Distance between Our Burdens and Ourselves

The time we spend with God will help us to put the necessary distance between what we feel and what is bothering us and dragging us down.

If we neglect to take the time needed, we run the risk of experiencing a spiritual standstill; a time when breaking through to God in our prayer costs us a tremendous effort. Stillness is rather like being on holiday—the distance between our everyday routine and ourselves helps us to find the way back to our inner selves and to the people we love. Far away from the hustle and anxieties of daily life, we have a wonderful time together, the best time of the year! There is no shortcut if you want to spend your 'holidays' with God.

Now see what effect these words written by Teresa of Avila have on you in the stillness. Let them just flow through your mind.

> Oh, Lord, you are my God.
> When you come to me,
> how can I doubt,
> that I may serve you?
> From henceforth I will forget myself,
> I shall have no other will
> than yours alone.
> My own desires have become without power over me.
> That which I can do; I can say 'yes',
> this is what I desire.[89]

Stage Three
Discovering the Regions of the Heart

A. Introduction

In present-day society, we are quick to associate the word 'heart' with feelings. It is often understood to mean a particular kind of mawkish or embarrassing sentimentality. The heart, or more to the point 'having a heart *for* something', is more likely to be associated with women than with men; possibly this is justifiable, as men very often find it difficult to reconcile the hectic schedule of everyday life and its external influences with their innermost feelings. It can be difficult for them to recognise the importance attached to the emotional function of the heart, and therefore difficult for them to utilise that function in a practical way.

The importance of the heart is commonly underestimated, so much so that we have no idea of how to put its resources to good use to create good works. The 'heart' is very often replaced by the 'head', the result being that we live passively rather than actively; our lives are lived out in our thoughts, and we cease to *feel* what life really is. We become easy prey for unpredictable powers and spirits, who interfere with our thoughts, sowing evil seeds and gradually taking over the helm. Finally, our own heart rebels against us and prevents us from exercising our own free will. You may then well ask: "What happened to the freedom we had in Christ?"

According to the Gospels, our heart reflects all our thoughts, feelings, wishes, dreams, what we say, what we set our minds on, and finally what we do. Jesus knows that acting upon the thoughts of an impure heart is the cause of all evil. That is why he said: "It is what comes out of a man that defiles him. For from inside, out of a man's heart, come evil thoughts, acts of fornication, of theft, murder, adultery, ruthless greed, and malice; fraud, indecency, envy, slander, arrogance, and folly; these evil things all come from inside, and they defile the man."[90]

Questions:
- *Are you aware of what is stirring in your heart during your time of stillness? If so, does it make you feel glad or does it shock you?*
- *To what extent are you aware of the functions of your heart? Are you aware of the potential involved?*

B. The Bible Passage

>>31. The time is coming, says the Lord, when I will make a new covenant with Israel and Judah. 32. It will not be like the covenant I made with their forefathers when I took them by the hand and led them out of Egypt. Although they broke my covenant, I was patient with them, says the Lord. 33. But this is the covenant which I will make with Israel after those days, says the Lord; I will set my law within them and write it on their hearts; I will become their God and they shall become my people.<< (Jer. 31: 31-33 The New English Bible; Oxford/Cambridge University Press 1970)

What Does the Passage Tell Us?

When God calls people to repent and change their ways, he speaks to the heart. The prophet Jeremiah was above all concerned with the 'attitude of heart' (as opposed to 'attitude of mind') amongst his contemporaries, as indeed were all the Biblical prophets. He reminded them that God expected them to have obedient hearts. Love, inward strength, the ability to hear his voice, accepting consolation, and many similar things are all virtues, which begin in the heart. Even faith comes from having briefly looked into God's heart and seen how he feels and thinks about mankind! It is God alone who initiates a change of heart resulting in a change of ways. By planting his Word and pouring out his Spirit in their hearts, he forms friendships with mere humans. He makes a covenant with them, which cannot be broken, not even when they leave this world and enter the next.

Johannes Kastl reminds us that our hearts can only become strong and steadfast through grace. He loved us first, when we did not love him, and through his boundless love, we receive grace in the form of a free pardon. The only force that will really change us is ". . . God's love (which) has flooded our innermost heart through the Holy Spirit He has given us."[91] We cherish indefinite hopes of being happier when we have overcome the difficulties and problems surrounding us. How many poor souls have capitulated after discovering that there is no therapist and no psychoanalyst who can guarantee them that elusive and much sought-after thing called happiness! Only a changed heart, a heart which is willing and prepared to do God's will, will give us the peace we desire. The reason for our difficulties is nearly always to be found in our not being able to make a categorical decision from the heart, because we only love God half-heartedly. The expression 'half-hearted' means exactly what it says: 'with half a heart'—without enthusiasm or effort—and that is where the danger lies in wait. The only remedy is to start going about things 'wholeheartedly'—completely and enthusiastically!

Questions:
- *Do you feel that as you continue to practise the Prayer of Stillness you are becoming more and more willing to accept inward changes in your life?*
- *Do you feel much more inclined to read the Bible, to keep times of fellowship with God, and to be kind and helpful to others?*
- *Are you aware of being strengthened day by day through your acceptance of God's love?*
- *Do you see what you would be capable of if only your will were set free to do it?*

C. Not Only "With All Your Mind" but "With All Your Heart"[92]

Since the Age of Enlightenment (also called the Age of Reason), in the eighteenth century, most of our thinking has been dominated by reason, at least in European society. We are constantly occupied with improving our knowledge in all directions. What we do *not* know is how to make the necessary changes to our own characters and in our own lives. We have isolated our hearts and become alienated from our own feelings; we have little chance of making any essential changes.

Do we have to stay that way? The heart should not be subjected by the mind; mind and heart should share a balanced existence. Knowledge should not be mistaken for faith! The heart should be mature enough to submit itself to God's Word. Only a mature heart can recognise and accept the authority of God's Word as it must be accepted.

One of the aims of the Prayer of Stillness is to help meditants develop the ability to return at any time, regardless of distractions and conflicts, to the inner state they experienced during the prayer itself when they were open to God's will and his presence. Only then will a person be able to return to that place of peace, trust God, and be able to hear his Word and act upon it whenever they wish or need to. A healthy mind will not disapprove of such an attitude; the mind will join the heart and put itself at God's disposal!

Questions:
- *Are you able to regain your sense of peace and the willingness to serve God in everyday situations? To what extent does the Prayer of Stillness help you?*
- *What influences your disposition or your present mood most? What things, people, or circumstances cause you to exercise your own will-power?*

D. A Major Misunderstanding

Bernard de Clairvaux wrote the following words about how difficult it is for the heart to open itself to God:

"What is a hardened heart? It is a heart which refuses to be rent by remorse, be softened by affection or be moved by pleading. It neither allows itself to be threatened, nor can it be impressed, . . . It is not grateful for good deeds and kindness, it does not accept advice, it is enraged when confronted with firm decisions, it does not shrink from being shameful, disgraceful and dishonourable.

It does not recognise danger, it does not understand human nature and therefore has no sympathy, it is indifferent to God. It immediately forgets the past, lives carelessly in the present, and is not concerned with the future. There is nothing which a hardened heart considers worth remembering except the insults it has been subjected to. It has nothing important to prepare itself for, either in the present or in the future, and nothing to look forward to, except when it is planning an act of revenge. To put all these horrific attributes in a nutshell; a hardened heart has forfeited the fear of God and all sensitivity to the feelings of others."[93]

Can we fail to recognise more than a just a hint of the present-day spirit of the times in Bernard de Clairvaux's words? Times change, but the human heart does not change. The Prayer of Stillness aims to help meditants find a way out of this hardness of heart.

Questions:
– *Do you recognise yourself in this description? Which points resemble your attitudes most?*
– *How does the Prayer of Stillness help you to discover your own hardness of heart and uncaring ways?*

Stage Four
Developing Your Own Vision

A. Introduction

The Prayer of Stillness puts us in the position of gradually being able to see the difference between what is important and what is not important more and more clearly. Have you ever wondered how you would use your strength and energy if you no longer had to pamper to obsessions or addictions and if you were no longer forced to be the slave of fear and sin? Please do not misunderstand me! I do not think that we will ever manage to lead an immaculate life with no problems while we abide here on this Earth, but that does not necessarily mean that we cannot go through periods of inner growth and change at various stages in life.

The Prayer of Stillness is not primarily concerned with 'doing', it has more to do with 'being' and with what we will eventually 'become' in Christ. Its chief contribution is that it sets free the forces within us, it awakens the energy and the will-power which will enable us to do whatever is necessary. We are usually capable of far more than we realise! What we tell those who begin somewhat late in life to realise just how much they are able to do is that it is never too late to begin with the important things, but it is a great pity if they never begin. It is a terrible waste and a shame that many do not even manage to set out on the path to find their own happiness and contentment in following Christ, let alone begin with their allotted task in life.

Activism—organising political or social changes—is often the driving factor, even in the church. More time spent in fellowship with God would serve a more useful purpose than does the developing of programmes, which might impress the general public but will almost certainly not win them for Christ.

The Carmelite Günter Becker wrote the following about the mystic John of the Cross:

"Juan (John) is totally convinced that love is the only thing that can change the world and mankind. He believes that only those who have been through the painful process of purification, and thus found love, will be able to achieve anything: 'Just a very small amount of such purified love is of more value to God and to a person's soul; is of more use to the church, than all other works put together.' We were, indeed, created for such love. Those so active ones amongst us should remember this while they are striving to conform to the world with their sermons and their outward works. They should remember that they would be of far more use to the church, and find far more favour with God, . . . if they were to spend just half of the time they spend on works in prayer and in God's presence, even if they have not yet attained that sublime state of grace which is being one with God. It is quite certain that they would achieve more through that one work; the work of their divinely-gifted prayer, than through a thousand other works."[94]

Questions:
- *Do you sometimes have the feeling that you have done something meaningful, something which pleases God? What causes that feeling?*
- *Is there something you have been wanting to do for a very long time to promote God's cause locally and worldwide, but as yet have not done?*

B. The Bible Passage
>>The Lord said to Joshua son of Nun, his assistant, '. . . 7. Only be strong and resolute; observe diligently all the law which my servant Moses has given you. You must not turn from it to right or left, if you would prosper wherever you go. 8. This book of the law must be ever on your lips; you must keep it in mind day and night so that you may diligently observe all that is written in it. Then you will prosper and be successful in all that you do. 9. This is my command: be strong, be resolute; do not be fearful or dismayed, for the Lord your God is with you wherever you go.' << (Josh. 1: 7-9 The New English Bible; Oxford/Cambridge University Press 1970)

What Does the Passage Tell Us?
God gave Joshua a very specific promise. That promise shows us that conquering and then possessing the country, which God had designated for his people was dependent upon his blessing, his help, and protection, and not on Joshua's skills in leadership. God is always the one behind the action when anything really important happens. God often chooses a particularly able person, such as

Moses or Joshua, to be the centre of attention, but it is God himself who acts. Joshua needed a very long time of preparation, just as Moses did, before he was ready to fulfil his task and lead Israel into the Promised Land. He spent years under the exemplary influence of Moses until he was ready and able to lead God's people to their destiny. The prerequisite was a well-developed sensitivity and a willing heart, things which Joshua had acquired during the long years. Is it surprising that one of God's conditions was that Joshua be willing to hear and obey his Word?

C. Our Time of Preparation

We sometimes assume that God must answer all our prayers instantly. We very often fail to see that there are certain preconditions, which must be met before God can act. From God's point of view not all of our intentions (no matter how well meant they are!) are worthy of being fulfilled spontaneously; we forget that God decides on place and time.

Some meditants might experience the time spent in the Prayer of Stillness as a time of preparation for things to come. If we rid ourselves of all fears, all false opinions, all flights of our imagination and all expectations, we will be inwardly prepared to hear the Word of Jesus Christ. Our spiritual eyes and our conscience will 'go into training' and we will learn to do without our own selfish ways.

The task we are being prepared for is very often something which we have always felt ourselves drawn to, for example, a person who feels a strong calling to help the underprivileged classes will remember that even as a child they had a strong desire to help those at a social disadvantage.

Question:
– Have you always felt drawn to a certain ministry? What is your special task?

D. Waiting for the Time to Be Right

God is omniscient. He knows everything, and so he has chosen the time and the circumstances for each of us to begin our life's task. We are in danger of succumbing to impatience along the way! We begin to think along the lines of: "While I'm waiting to do something really important, I might not realise that what I am already doing is important!" We might even miss the opportunity of doing something really important for God because we are too busy concentrating on our own selves. We must be careful not to live in constant fear that we will not have enough time left here on Earth to do whatever it is that we are supposed do. God has given us our time here on Earth, and he knows how much we need. Our part is to stay close to God, to listen out for his voice, and to be ready to do what he tells us to do, when he tells us.

Questions:
– *Do you believe that you must have missed some opportunities in the past? Does that make you feel unhappy?*
– *Are there times when you think about the future and become impatient? What are you most afraid of? Why?*

E. Caring for Your Neighbours

Meditants will notice that they are united with the will of Christ in caring and providing for those of their fellow beings who are in need. The Prayer of Stillness will achieve its objectives by helping us to minister to the people around us, especially to those who are needy. This is an integral part of our calling. Jesus said: "Go forth to every part of the world, and proclaim the Good News to the whole creation."[95] It is up to God to decide what he wants us to do, and he will complete the task he gives us *through us*, just as he did with Joshua.

Questions:
– Have you noticed that the more you grow to love God, the more you are drawn into caring for others?
– To what extent are you moved by the people in need who you see around you, and by the enormous number of needy people in this world?

F. Make Your Vision Grow!

The Prayer of Stillness will gradually make you realise that you have sufficient strength and energy to complete your life's work and to carry out the special task you were created for.

If possible, you should join forces with others who are like-minded, develop a plan to share your ministries, and then work together. If our expectations are too great in this point, we will be brought back down to earth by reality, and it will be easier to change our original plans accordingly.

In most cases, we are able to do more than we ever imagined, provided our strength and energy are set free to do God's will. Once we have begun, we will notice that we strive and wish for nothing other than for those things, which are God's will.

Start out on the path back to God's heart today!

In the stillness, ponder over the following words:

Lord, in the *I am* which is your essence,
I have seen the essence of all truth.
YOU are the *I am* which has no beginning and no end.
All other *beings* have their source in YOUR *being*.
YOU are the love from which all else was created.
YOU are the glory from which all glory flows.[96]

Bibliography

A. J. Appasamy, *What Shall We Believe* (Madras: C.L.S. Press, 1992).

Günter Benker, *Loslassen können—die Liebe finden* (Letting go—Finding Love) (Grünewald, 1991).

Der Sadhu, *Christliche Mystik in einer indischen Seele, Verlag Friedrich Andreas Perthes A-G—Stuttgart* (Gotha, 1923).

Klaus Berger, *Was ist biblische Spiritualität* (What is Biblical Spirituality?) (Gütersloh: *Quell/Gütersloher Verlagshaus*, 2000).

Benedikt von Canfield, *Regel der Vollkommenheit* (The Rules of Perfection) (Dietrich-Kolde-Verlag, 1989).

Jean Pierre de Caussade, *The Sacrament of the Present Moment* (New York: Harper Collins, 1982).

Bernhard de Clairvaux, *Sämtliche Werke 1* (Complete Works I) (Innsbruck: Tyrolia Verlag, 1990).

Bernhard de Clairvaux, *Rückkehr zu Gott* (Returning to God) (Die mystische Schriften, Patmos Verlag, Düsseldorf, 2006).

Peter Dyckhoff, *Einübung in das Ruhegebet* (Practising the Prayer of Stillness) (Eine christliche Praxis nach Johannes Cassian, Don Bosco, Münschen, 2006).

Friedrich Heiler, Sadhu Sundar Singh, *Ein Apostel des Ostens und Westens* (Friedrich Reinhard/Basel, 1926).

Maximilino Herraiz-Garcia, *Beten mit Hl. Teresa* (The Prayers of St Teresa) (Herder, Freiburg, 1987).

William Ralph Inge, *Christian Mysticism* (The Project Gutenberg eBook, 2005).

Thomas R. Kelly, *A Testament of Devotion* (San Francisco: Harper, 1996).

Francisco de Osuna, *Versenkung* (Contemplation), Weg und Weisung des Kontemplatives Gebets, (Herder, Freiburg, 1984).

Friso Melzer, *Versenkung oder Begegnung* (Contemplation or Encounter) (Stuttgart: Evangelischer Missionsverlag, 1987).

Friso Melzer, *Innerung, Wege und Stufen der Meditation* (Inward Expression; Ways and Levels of Life) (Kassel: Johannes Stauda Verlag, 1977).

Thomas Merton, *No Man is an Island* (New York: A Harvest/HBJ Book, 1983).

Thomas Merton, *Contemplative Prayer* (Michigan: Cistercian Publications, 1971).

Michael Molinos, *The Spiritual Guide* (Jacksonwille: Christian Books Publishing House Wilfrid Stinissen, *Ewigkeit mitten in der Zeit* (Eternity in My Time) (Mainz: Matthias-Grünewald, 2002).

Gerhard Tersteegen, *Weg der Wahrheit* (The Way of Truth) (Stuttgart: J. F. Steinkopf Verlag, 1968).

Johannes Tauler, *Das Reich Gottes in uns* (The Kingdom of God Within Us) (München: Drei Eichen Verlag, 1982).

Johannes Tauler, *Sermons* (New York: Paulist Press, 1985).

Grundkurs Spiritualität des Karmel Hersg Michael Platten und Elisabeth Hense, 2006 (Verlag Katholisches Bibelwerk, Stuttgart).

Endnotes

1 Colossians 2: 2 (The New English Bible; Oxford/Cambridge University Press, 1970)
2 Psalm 37: 7 (King James Bible)
3 Isaiah 30: 15 (The New English Bible; Oxford/Cambridge University Press, 1970)
4 I Kings 19: 11-13 (The New English Bible; Oxford/Cambridge University Press, 1970)
5 ,Versenkung'('Contemplation') by Francisco de Osuna. Page 85.
6 Matthew 4: 1-11 and Luke 4: 1-13
7 Mark 1: 35
8 Luke 14: 33 (The New English Bible; Oxford/Cambridge University Press, 1970) (See also The King James Bible: "So likewise, whosoever he be of you that forsaketh not all that he hath, he cannot be my disciple.")
9 Galatians 1: 17
10 There is no such word as 'meditant' in the English or the German language. I have taken it from the French. It means 'he/she who meditates'. In the Prayer of Stillness the meditant is urged on by a powerful need to seek (and find) God. The act of praying consists of an attitude of the heart rather than consisting of spoken words or thoughts.
11 Galatians 2: 20
12 Luke 10: 27
13 The word 'self-denial' in this sense does not refer to a 'loss', but rather to a 'gain'. It means something which for us seems to be absolutely contrary to our inclinations. Turning our backs on all material things does not come naturally to us. What these non-essentials really do is to distract us from the essentials, even though what we expect of them is happiness. What better reason do we need for neglecting or even forgetting them? We can then move on towards the more important things; towards the essentials. Those who set out resolutely on the path of self-denial will quite certainly come to terms with themselves and with God, and at the same time find peace and happiness. Jesus was the one who always found his way back to the essentials, because he denied himself. Those who follow in his footsteps fulfil his words: "Whosoever will come after me, let him deny himself, and take up his cross, and follow me." Mark 8: 34 (King James Bible).
14 Johannes Cassianus (Johannes of Massilia) lived from 360 to 435 AD. He was a Christian priest, monk, abbot and writer. Cassian's writings belong to the most important early Christian theological works. Numerous theologians have been influenced by them, including Thomas à Kempis.

15 Ephesians 5: 14 (King James Bible). The New English Bible; Oxford/ Cambridge University Press 1970 translates as follows: "Awake sleeper, rise from the dead, and Christ will shine upon you."

16 John 3, 20, and 21 (The New English Bible; Oxford/Cambridge University Press, 1970)

17 1. John 2: 11 (The New English Bible; Oxford/Cambridge University Press, 1970)

18 ,Weg der Wahrheit' ('The Way of Truth') by Gerhard Tersteegen. Page 32.

19 John 1: 9 (The New English Bible; Oxford/Cambridge University Press, 1970)

20 2 Corinthians 4: 6 (King James Bible)

21 Exodus 13: 21

22 John 3: 21 (The New English Bible; Oxford/Cambridge University Press, 1970)

23 ,Wege und Stufen der Meditation' ('Ways and Stages of Meditation') by Friso Melzer. Pages 74 and 75.

24 2 Chronicles 7: 14 "If my people which are called by my name shall humble themselves, and pray, and seek my face, and turn from their wicked ways; then I will hear from heaven, and will forgive their sin, and will heal their land." (King James Bible).

25 Philippians 2: 7 (The New English Bible; Oxford/Cambridge University Press, 1970)

26 Source unknown.

27 'Contemplation' is understood to mean; 'seeing and perceiving spiritual things with the heart.'

28 'What Shall We Believe?' by A.J.Appasamy. Page 7.

29 ,Das Reich Gottes in uns' ('The Kingdom of God Within Us') by Johannes Tauler. Page 174.

30 ,Ewigkeit mitten in meiner Zeit' ('Eternity in My Time') by Wilfrid Stinissen. Page 30.

31 James 1: 14 (The New English Bible; Oxford/Cambridge University Press, 1970 and King James Bible).

32 ,Regel der Vollkommenheit' ('The Rules of Perfection') by Benedict von Canfield. Page 133.

33 Zechariah 1: 3 taken from James 4: 8 (The New English Bible; Oxford/ Cambridge University Press, 1970)

34 ,Versenkung' ('Contemplation') by Francisco de Osuna. Page 34.

35 Luke 8: 21 (The New English Bible; Oxford/Cambridge University Press, 1970)

36 John 14: 23 (The New English Bible; Oxford/Cambridge University Press, 1970)

37 ,Beten mit Hl. Teresa' ('The Prayers of St Teresa') Published by Herder. Page 170.

38 'No Man is an Island' by Thomas Merton. Page 105.
39 ,Innerungen; Wege und Stufen des Lebens' ('Inward Expression; Ways and Stages of Life') by Friso Melzer. Page 82.
40 I Kings 18: 21 (The New English Bible; Oxford/Cambridge University Press, 1970)
41 Genesis 4: 7 (King James Bible) More modern translations do not have the same text.
42 1 Peter 5: 10 (The New English Bible; Oxford/Cambridge University Press, 1970)
43 When God appeared to Moses on Horeb, the mountain of God, he answered the question as to his name with the words: "I AM; that is who I am. Tell them that 'I AM' has sent you to them." Exodus 3: 14 (The New English Bible; Oxford/Cambridge University Press, 1970). When we become aware of his presence, we will be able to hear and obey him.
44 Mark 4: 12 (The New English Bible; Oxford/Cambridge University Press, 1970).
45 Hebrews 3: 7 (The New English Bible; Oxford/Cambridge University Press, 1970).
46 Revelation 3: 20
47 ,Ewigkeit mitten in meiner Zeit' ('Eternity in My Time') by Wilfrid Stinissen. Page 26.
48 'Sermons' by Johannes Tauler. Pages 46 and 47. Not translated; English original.
49 'Sermons' by Johannes Tauler. Page 47. Not translated; English original.
50 Philippians 2: 7 (The New English Bible; Oxford/Cambridge University Press, 1970)
51 John 14, 23
52 ,Was ist biblischer Spiritualität?' ('What is Biblical Spirituality?') by Klaus Berger. Page 70.
53 ,Was ist biblischer Spiritualität?' ('What is Biblical Spirituality?') by Klaus Berger. Page 73.
54 Bernard de Clairvaux; ,Sämtliche Werke I' ('Complete Works I') Page 225.
55 ,Loslassen können, die Liebe finden' ('Letting Go and Finding Love') by Günter Benker. Page 53.
56 Matthew 4: 3 (The New English Bible; Oxford/Cambridge University Press, 1970)
57 Romans 8: 14 -16
58 Philippians 2: 13
59 ,Versenkung oder Begegnung' ('Contemplation or Encounter') by Friso Melzer. Page 48.
60 'Contemplative Prayer' by Thomas Merton. Page 22.

61 'The Sadhu, Christian Mysticism in an Indian Soul.' by A. J. Appasamy. Page 142.

62 W. R. Inge quotes from Richard of St. Viktor; a 12th century mystic. 'Christian Mysticism' by William Ralph Inge; 2005. Page 14.

63 'Sadhu Sundar Singh' by Friedrich Heiler. Page 81.

64 Bernard de Clairvaux; ,Sämtliche Werke I' ('Complete Works I') Page 143

65 Zechariah 7: 5

66 'Guia Espiritual' by Miguel de Molinos. Page 83. See also 1 John 3: 18: "My children, must not be a matter of words or talk; it must be genuine and show itself in action."(The New English Bible; Oxford/Cambridge University Press, 1970)

67 'The Sacrament of the Present Time' by Jean Pierre de Caussade. Page 70.

68 Matthew 6: 7

69 Matthew 6: 6b (The New English Bible; Oxford/Cambridge University Press, 1970)

70 Mark 7: 20-23 (The New English Bible; Oxford/Cambridge University Press, 1970)

71 Isaiah 50: 2

72 1 Thessalonians 5: 16-18a

73 Psalm 139

74 Matthew 12: 44

75 Ephesians 2: 10 (The New English Bible; Oxford/Cambridge University Press, 1970)

76 'Sadhu Sundar Singh', by F. Heiler. Page 85.

77 ,Versenkung' ('Contemplation') by Francisco de Osuna. Page 131.

78 This is the second verse of the Lord's Prayer and is to be found in Matthew chapter 6, verse 10.

79 ,Versenkung' ('Contemplation') by Francisco de Osuna. Page 85.

80 Jeremiah 29: 11

81 Luke 12: 15 (The New English Bible; Oxford/Cambridge University Press, 1970) The translation given in the King James Bible reads as follows: "... for a man's life consisteth not in the abundance of the things which he possesseth."

82 ,Rückkehr zu Gott' ('Returning to God') by Bernard de Clairvaux, Patmos Publishings. Page 92.

83 Luke 9: 23 (The New English Bible; Oxford/Cambridge University Press, 1970)

84 ,Aufstieg zum Berg Karmel', Johannes vom Kreuz ('Ascending Mount Carmel'; John of the Cross). Quotation taken from ,Loslassen können' ('Being Able to Let Go') by Günter Benker. Page 82.

85 Matt 16, 25

86 Matthew 10: 30

87 Romans 8: 28

88 Jeremiah 31: 13
89 Taken from ‚Verweilen bei einem Freund' ('Time Spent with a Friend') Prayers by Teresa of Avila. Published by Verlag Neue Stadt. Page 75.
90 Mark 7: 20-22. (The New English Bible; Oxford/Cambridge University Press 1970)
91 Romans 5: 5 (The New English Bible; Oxford/Cambridge University Press 1970)
92 Matthew 22: 37
93 ‚Rückkehr zu Gott' ('Returning to God') by Bernard de Clairvaux, Patmos Publishings. Page 75.
94 ‚Loslassen können, die Liebe finden' ('Letting Go and Finding Love') by Günter Benker. Page 131.
95 Mark 16: 15-16
96 Einübung in das Ruhegebet' ('Practising the Prayer of Stillness') by Peter Dyckhoff. Page 83.